THE CHILDREN'S
ATLAS OF PEOPLE & PLACES

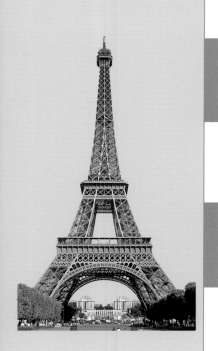

THE CHILDREN'S ATLAS OF PEOPLE & PLACES

TRAVEL THE WORLD AND VISIT PEOPLE IN FAR-OFF LANDS

JENNY WOOD

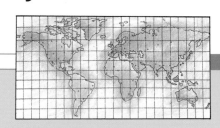

The Millbrook Press
Brookfield, Ct.

A QUARTO BOOK

First published in the United States of America in 1993 by
The Millbrook Press Inc.
2 Old New Milford Road
Brookfield, Connecticut 06804.

Library of Congress Cataloging-in-Publication Data

Wood, Jenny.
    The children's atlas of people and places/by Jenny Wood and
David Munro.
       p.   cm.
    Includes index.
    Summary: Maps, facts, and illustrations present the diverse places
and people on our planet.
      ISBN 1–56294–712–5 (trade ed.), ISBN 1–56294–257–3 (lib. ed.), ISBN 1–56294–926–8 (club ed.)
      1. Atlases. [1. Atlases] I. Munro, David, Dr. II. Title.
G1021.W645 1993 <G&M>
912–dc20   92–28857
                                         CIP
                                    MAP AC

This book was designed and produced by
Quarto Publishing plc
The Old Brewery, 6 Blundell Street, London N7 9BH

Consultant David Munro
Creative Director Nick Buzzard
Senior Editor Cynthia O'Brien
Editors Marilyn Inglis, Sean Connolly
Design Assistant Trish Going
Maps Janos Marffy
Illustrator Jim Robins
Picture Research Louise Edgeworth, Liz Eddison

The Publishers would like to thank the following for their help in the
preparation of this book: Malcolm Porter (Contour), Karen Ball,
Julian Ewart.

Typeset by Proteus Typesetters, Worle, England
Manufactured by Bright Arts Singapore (Pte) Ltd
Printed by Star Standard (Pte) Ltd, Singapore
Library binding in USA by Horowitz/Rae Book Manufacturers, Inc.

CONTENTS

SECTION 1: INTRODUCTION

The first human beings appeared about half a million years ago. Despite the fact that people have changed the face of the Earth with farms, cities, and national boundaries, it retains the power to challenge as well as nourish the billions of people who live on it.

THE PLANET AND ITS PEOPLE

The Children's Atlas of People and Places provides a fascinating portrait of a planet that retains its enduring features while changing every second. The Earth seems largely unchanged in the course of a brief human lifetime. The shapes and familiar features of the continents remain the same. Earthquakes, volcanic eruptions, and geysers show us that the Earth is still evolving, but the overall picture is constant.

At the same time there is truth to the old saying that the world is getting smaller. Modern transportation and communications make natural boundaries seem less important. The two-month transatlantic voyage of Christopher Columbus in 1492 could be made today in about four hours by Concorde.

This atlas paints a picture of the constantly changing human influence on the Earth. New countries emerge or gain their freedom; other countries subdivide, join together or change their names.

Ultimately, people affect not just the boundaries that they draw, but the Earth itself. Industrial pollution, damage to the ozone layer, and the destruction of the tropical rain forests are serious threats to the Earth's future. The human race needs to channel its curiosity and inventiveness to protect the planet that provides its home.

Left The Chrysler Building soars above the New York skyline. A fine example of Art Deco style, it is surrounded by many other skyscrapers.

Below Thousands of commuters pass through Liverpool Street Railway Station in England each day. Modern cities need efficient transportation systems so that people can get to work quickly.

Left A group of Mexicans poses for a photograph during a family celebration. Extended families are important in many parts of the world. Children often live with their grandparents, aunts, and uncles.

Right Tourists take up all the available space along the beach at Gijon in northwest Spain. Some European beaches are becoming overcrowded.

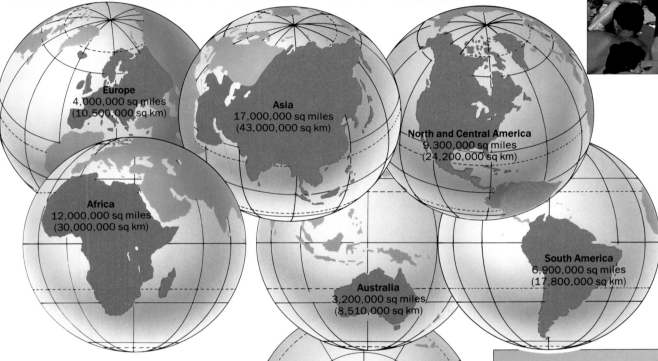

Europe
4,000,000 sq miles
(10,500,000 sq km)

Asia
17,000,000 sq miles
(43,000,000 sq km)

North and Central America
9,300,000 sq miles
(24,200,000 sq km)

Africa
12,000,000 sq miles
(30,000,000 sq km)

South America
6,900,000 sq miles
(17,800,000 sq km)

Australia
3,200,000 sq miles
(8,510,000 sq km)

Antarctica
5,500,000 sq miles
(14,250,000 sq km)

Above The continents as shown on the globes indicate that Asia is by far the largest continent. It takes up nearly a third of the total land area of the world. Africa, the next in size, is two thirds as large as Asia. North America and South America are third and fourth largest. Antarctica, by the South Pole, is fifth largest. Europe (sixth) and Australia (seventh) are about the same size, but Europe has about 20 times as many people.

Right Traditional fishing villages still line the shores of most European countries along the Mediterranean.

An explosion of people

People often speak about a world "population explosion" that could threaten the survival of the human race and the Earth itself. The evidence shows that the world population has not only been rising, but that the increase has been accelerating. In 1850 there were 1.18 billion people, and the figure rose to 1.6 billion by 1900. But experts predict that the world population in the year 2000 will exceed 6 billion — five times the population of 1850.

1850

1900

2000

CLIMATE

People have inhabited six of the Earth's seven continents for thousands of years. During that time they have had to adapt to the patterns of temperature and weather conditions that are typical of their own region. These patterns are known as climate.

A region's climate depends partly on how far north or south it is from the Equator, an imaginary line that circles the Earth midway between the two poles. As a rule, regions near the Equator are the hottest places, while those near the poles are the coldest.

Other factors play a part in forming an area's climate. Regions near the sea generally have more rainfall and less variation in temperature than inland areas. Cooler conditions prevail at higher altitudes.

Most of the world has one of the nine regional climates described on these pages.

Polar and tundra areas, in the extreme polar regions have temperatures that rarely rise above freezing. The North (right) and South poles are covered in ice that is several hundreds of yards thick. Land masses near the poles are cold, dry plains, where only mosses and lichens can grow.

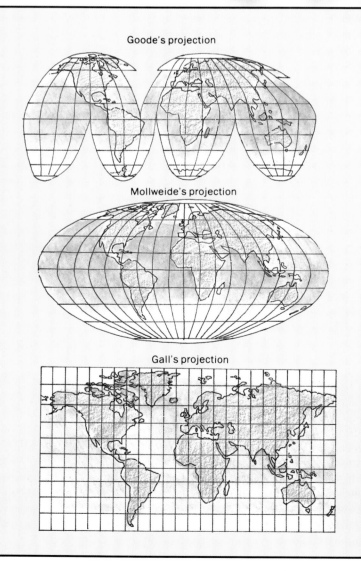

Flattening the Earth

Modern mapmakers use one of three projections to represent the Earth. Each must distort the round shape in order to show familiar areas. *Goode's projection* "peels" the Earth in the way that we peel an orange. Distances remain accurate but there are gaps where the Earth narrows near the poles. *Mollweide's projection* fills in those gaps by treating the world as one curve. Places near the center are distorted least. *Gall's projection*, used in this book, treats the Earth like a cylinder. It unwraps in the way a soup can label comes off. These maps are good for portraying regions but Gall's projection of the whole world stretches the extreme north and south to make them appear much wider than they really are.

Goode's projection

Mollweide's projection

Gall's projection

Mountain regions have a type of climate that is defined more by altitude than by distance from the Equator. Above a certain height, called the tree line, mountain conditions become too cold to support vegetation. Some mountains along the Equator, such as the Andes, are covered in snow all year long.

Taiga regions in northern Canada, Scandinavia, and Siberia have short summers and long, cold winters. They are covered by evergreen forests, because deciduous trees cannot survive the severe winters. The Russian word *taiga*, meaning "marshy forest," describes this type of climate.

Temperate forests cover many parts of North America and northern Asia where there is regular rainfall and temperatures are never too extreme. These forests have deciduous trees, which grow new leaves each year. The productive farming regions of northern Europe were once covered by similar forests.

Mediterranean areas along the Mediterranean Sea (above) have hot, dry summers and mild, wet winters. Similar conditions exist in California, southern Africa, and Australia, regions that have successfully introduced Mediterranean crops such as citrus fruits, grapes, and olives.

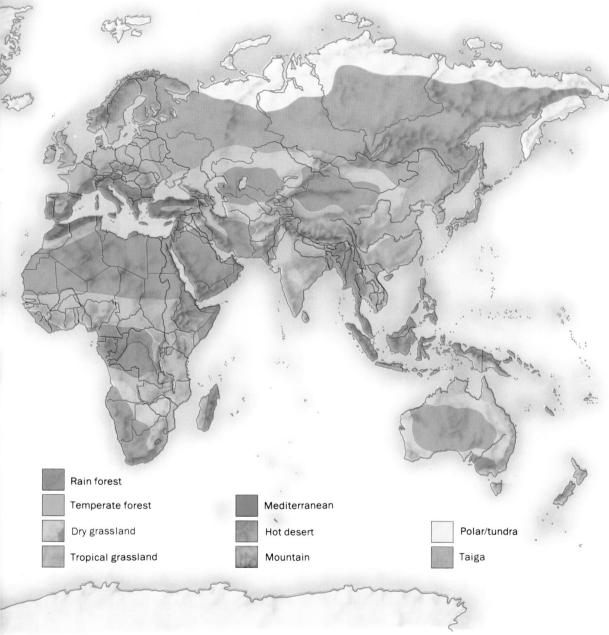

Rain forest

Temperate forest

Dry grassland

Tropical grassland

Mediterranean

Hot desert

Mountain

Polar/tundra

Taiga

Dry grasslands experience climates of extreme heat and cold because they are far from the sea. The rich soil of these grasslands, which include the North American prairies and the Russian steppes, makes them ideal for growing grain and raising large herds of cattle.

Tropical rain forests are low-lying regions around the Equator that are hot and wet throughout the year. Dense rain forests, such as those of central Africa and the Amazon Basin (left), cover these regions. They are home to the world's widest variety of plant and animal life.

Tropical grasslands border many rain forests. They are just as hot, but receive most of their rainfall in a six-month rainy season. Lions, zebras (right), and elephants thrive among the tall grasses and low trees of Africa's grasslands, also known as the savannah.

Hot deserts are also near the Equator, but receive little or no rainfall to modify the extreme heat. Parts of the Sahara (above), the Australian Outback, and Chile's Atacama Desert go years without any rain. Only highly adapted plants and animals survive in these harsh regions.

THE EARTH'S RESOURCES

The world depends on natural resources for food, to produce energy, and to manufacture goods. Some countries, such as the United States, have a wide range of these resources. Others, including those in the desert regions of Africa, have very few. Still others, such as the oil-producing regions of the Middle East, have one major resource but few others.

People are constantly looking for ways to develop these resources. Minerals used in industry, and fuels such as coal, oil, and natural gas, lie beneath the Earth's surface.

Important food crops and pasture land for livestock depend on particular types of soil.

Climate is also important. Coffee, tea, and cocoa can only grow in warm, tropical climates. Many cereals and grains need a cooler climate to thrive. Even water is a natural resource. It can provide hydro-electric energy as well as turn desert regions into productive farmland.

Above The United States has nearly 100 million head of cattle, more than any other country. Most of the cattle are raised on large ranches in the West and Southwest, such as this longhorn cattle ranch in Utah.

Right Workers spread beans for drying on a coffee plantation in Guyana. South America produces more coffee than any other region in the world. New varieties are constantly introduced in order to improve quality and output.

Right The symbols on the map indicate the distribution of natural resources around the world. Some countries are well endowed with many resources while others have very few — distribution is by no means equal.

Left Wheat is one of the world's most important food-producing grains. It grows best in the rich soil of the plains that lie in the center of several continents.

Right Excess gas is burned off at an oil field in Saudi Arabia. The Middle East region has the world's largest reserves of this precious energy resource.

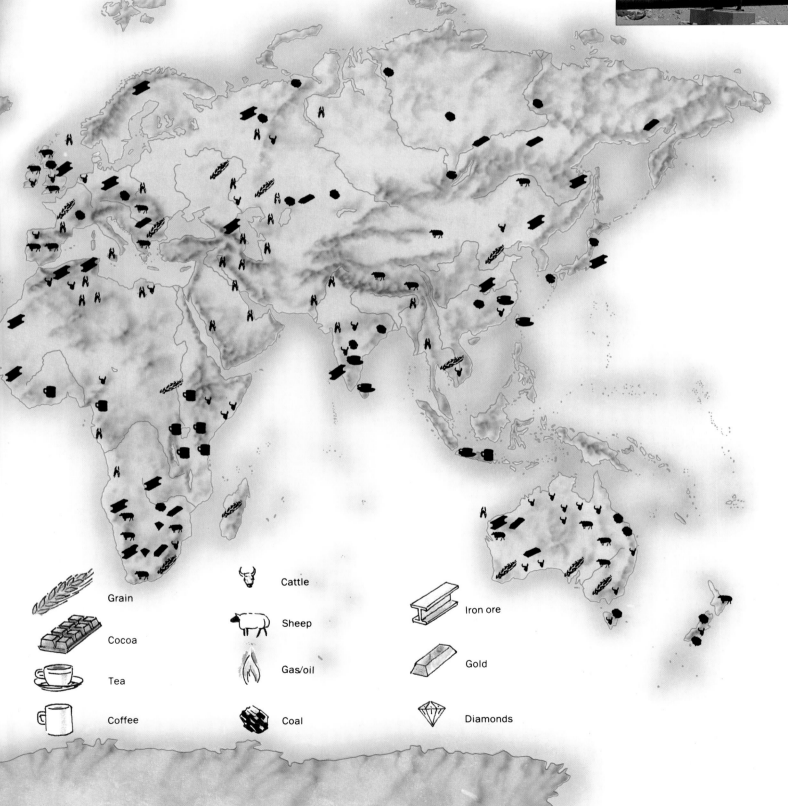

Grain

Cocoa

Tea

Coffee

Cattle

Sheep

Gas/oil

Coal

Iron ore

Gold

Diamonds

Above The Great Wall of China was one of the most effective and impressive physical borders ever constructed.

Right A group of people play cards outside a border post on the boundary between Sharjah and Dubai. These two states are part of the United Arab Emirates in the Middle East. Border posts between friendly neighbors help keep track of the flow of people and trade between the two countries. Customs and immigration officials check passports and commercial documents.

THE POLITICAL WORLD

The world is divided into many different countries, each with its own culture and system of government. Countries vary greatly in size and population. China, Asia's giant, has more than 1.1 billion people. Nauru, a small Pacific island country, has only 8,000. Australia occupies an entire continent but its population is less than that of the state of New York.

The boundaries between countries can be either natural, like a river, mountain range, or lake, or artificial. This second type of boundary, like that between Canada and the United States, is simply a line drawn across a map. Boundaries often change because of wars or diplomatic agreement. A look at a map of Eastern Europe or Africa 10, 50, or 100 years ago would show very different national boundaries from those of today.

The map opposite shows how the world is divided into countries. Even as this book goes to press, there are disputes going on over the borders of former Yugoslavia. Czechoslovakia is now split in two.

GREENLAND

ALASKA (US)

CANADA

UNITED STATES OF AMERICA

MEXICO

BAHAMAS
DOMINICAN REPUBLIC
CUBA
ST. KITTS & NEVIS
HAITI
ANTIGUA & BARBUDA
BELIZE JAMAICA ST. LUCIA DOMINICA
GUATEMALA HONDURAS BARBADOS
ST. VINCENT & GRENADA
EL SALVADOR NICARAGUA GRENADINES
COSTA RICA PANAMA TRINIDAD & TOBAGO
VENEZUELA
GUIN
GUYANA
SURINAME
COLOMBIA FRENCH GUIANA

ECUADOR

PERU
BRAZIL

BOLIVIA

PARAGUAY

URUGUAY

CHILE ARGENTINA

Left The Berlin Wall divided the city for nearly 30 years. It was built in 1961 when Berlin and Germany were divided into East and West. The Wall divided families and was a symbol of the division of Europe itself. In 1989 people were allowed free access through the Berlin Wall. Berliners celebrated in 1990 when Germany was reunified and the Wall was destroyed.

CAMEROON
Capital: Yaoundé
Population: 11,900,000

Throughout this book you will find flags of countries. Next to the flag is the name of the country, the name of the capital city, and the population of the country.

1 LIECHTENSTEIN
2 ANDORRA
3 MONACO
4 LUXEMBOURG
5 SAN MARINO
6 VATICAN CITY
7 SLOVENIA
8 CROATIA
9 YUGOSLAVIA
10 BOSNIA & HERCEGOVINA
11 ALBANIA
12 MACEDONIA
13 NETHERLANDS
14 SERBIA
15 MONTENEGRO

SECTION 2: EUROPE

Europeans live in a continent that is full of variety and contrasts. The people provide some of this variety, with their dozens of languages and different cultures. The land plays a part, too, from Arctic snowfields to the heat of the Mediterranean.

INTRODUCTION

About 700 million people, one seventh of the world's population, live in the 49 countries that make up the continent of Europe. About 50 different languages are spoken.

The landscape of Europe is as varied as its people. Rolling hills and fertile plains in the central areas lie between mountains and forests in the north and south. Most European countries have a coastline ranging

Above Tourists and office workers relax in Trafalgar Square near Nelson's Column, in the heart of London's busy West End. Big Ben at the Palace of Westminster looms in the distance.

Below The Eiffel Tower has dominated the Paris skyline since 1889, when it was erected to mark the centenary of the French Revolution. It is an iron framework rising 984 ft (300 m). Lifts go to a viewing deck near the top.

ICELAND
NORWAY
FINLAND
SWEDEN
ESTONIA
LATVIA
UNITED KINGDOM
DENMARK
LITHUANIA
IRELAND
RUSSIAN FEDERATION
NETHERLANDS
POLAND
BELARUS
BELGIUM
GERMANY
LUXEMBOURG
CZECHOSLOVAKIA
LIECHTENSTEIN
UKRAINE
SWITZERLAND
AUSTRIA
HUNGARY
MOLDOVA
FRANCE
ROMANIA
MONACO
SAN MARINO
ANDORRA
YUGOSLAVIA
BULGARIA
PORTUGAL
SPAIN
ITALY
GEORGIA
ALBANIA
GREECE
MALTA

Left The whitewashed cottages of La Irvela cling to the hills that rise from Granada in southern Spain. La Irvela was built by the Moors, who ruled most of Spain for 700 years.

from the rain-washed shores of western Ireland and the mighty Norwegian fjords to the sun-baked fishing villages of Greece.

About half of Europe's land is used for farming, and agriculture provides employment for around one sixth of the population. Many parts of Europe are heavily industrialized, and the continent is now the world's leading producer of manufactured goods. Europe is also rich in coal, iron ore, natural gas, and petroleum.

In 1945, after World War II, the countries of Europe were divided between East and West, but today these divisions are disappearing. The twelve countries of the European Community (EC) aim to enlarge the membership of the Community to embrace all the countries of Europe.

Below The fairy-tale turrets of Neuschwanstein Castle soar toward the peaks of the Bavarian Alps in southern Germany. Despite its medieval appearance, the castle is only about 100 years old. King Ludwig II of Bavaria almost went bankrupt when he built it to celebrate his reign.

THE COUNTRIES OF EUROPE

—— 16 ——
Andorra, Portugal, Spain

—— 18 ——
British Isles

—— 20 ——
Belgium, France, Luxembourg, Monaco, Netherlands

—— 22 ——
Austria, Germany, Liechtenstein, Switzerland

—— 24 ——
Czechoslovakia, Poland

—— 26 ——
Bulgaria, Hungary, Romania

—— 28 ——
Albania, Greece, Italy, Malta, San Marino, Vatican City, Yugoslavia

—— 30 ——
Denmark, Finland, Iceland, Norway, Sweden

—— 32 ——
Belarus, Estonia, Georgia, Latvia, Lithuania, Moldova, Russia, Ukraine

miles
0   1000
0   1000
kilometers

Left The Colosseum is Rome's great landmark. More than 100,000 spectators in 80 BC could see gladiators, exotic animals, and mock naval battles when the arena was flooded.

Right Dancers celebrate the Rite of Spring in Liepaja, a town on Latvia's Baltic coast. An image representing winter is burned by dancers dressed in the bright colors of spring. The custom is centuries old.

SPAIN AND PORTUGAL

Spain and Portugal make up the Iberian Peninsula in the southwest corner of Europe. Spain is the third largest country in Europe and since 1950 has fast developed into an industrial nation. Portugal, by contrast, is still largely rural. Two thirds of its population live in villages and earn a living by either farming or fishing.

The center of Spain consists of a hot, dry plateau called the Meseta. To the north and south are snowcapped mountain ranges. Fertile farmland is found around the coast, where Spain's thriving tourist industry is concentrated. The Tagus River divides Portugal's hilly north from the flatter, and drier, south.

Farming is an important part of life. Citrus fruits, olives, and wheat are grown in Spain, while Portugal produces olive oil and cork. Both countries export large quantities of the wine they produce.

On the southern tip of Spain lies the British dependency of Gibraltar. Andorra, one of the smallest countries in the world, nestles high in the Pyrenees, in the north-east corner of Spain.

Left The sway of colorful frilled dresses accompanies the lively rhythm of the Sevillianas, the dance of Seville. Many Spanish cities have given their names to special dances, which develop from local folk music. Guitars and castanets provide the melody and rhythm.

Parades of the faithful

The Spanish and Portuguese people hold many Roman Catholic festivals. St. James Day is celebrated here in the streets of Santiago de Compostela, which has been a place of pilgrimage for centuries. Solemn processions are organized during Holy Week–the week before Easter. People often carry statues of the Virgin Mary and the saints through the streets.

Left Whitewashed holiday homes overlook the fishing boats on the beach at Praia de Carvoeiro, in Portugal's Algarve province. The Algarve, on Portugal's southern coast, is one of Europe's leading tourist destinations.

Right The church of the Sagrada Familia, or Holy Family, is one of Barcelona's most famous landmarks. Designed by the eccentric Catalan architect Anton Gaudi, it remained unfinished when he died in 1926.

ANDORRA
Capital: Andorra-la-Vella
Population: 60,000

GIBRALTAR
Capital: Gibraltar
Population: 29,692

PORTUGAL
Capital: Lisbon
Population: 10,528,000

SPAIN
Capital: Madrid
Population: 39,623,000

Bay of Biscay

La Coruna • Santander • San Sebastian

Cantabria Mts. • Bilbao

ATLANTIC OCEAN • Vigo

Pyrenees

Pico de Aneto ▲ Andorra-la-Vella ◻

ANDORRA

Burgos

Valladolid • Duero • Ebro • Zaragoza

Serranía de Cuenca

Barcelona •

Sierra de Gredos

S P A I N

Madrid ◻

Tagus

P O R T U G A L

Porto •

BALEARIC ISLANDS

MINORCA

MAJORCA

Valencia •

IBIZA

◻ Lisbon

Guadiana

Setubal

Sierra Morena

Cordoba •

Guadalquivir

Murcia •

MEDITERRANEAN SEA

Seville •

Algarve

Granada •

Sierra Nevada ▲ Mulhacen

Malaga •

Costa del Sol

Cadiz •

• Gibraltar (U.K.)

miles
0 ——————— 100
0 ——————— 100
kilometers

MADEIRA

Madeira is the largest of a group of Portuguese islands lying off the African coast. Sea breezes give Madeira a mild climate all year long, making the island ideal for growing flowers and producing wine.

Above Small farms are common in Spain despite the country's recent industrial development. This farmer in Alicante uses a traditional horse-drawn plow to work his small fields.

Left Puerto Ducesa is a luxury resort on the Costa del Sol, Spain's "Sun Coast" on the Mediterranean. Many former fishing villages have become bustling tourist centers in the last 30 years.

Bullfighting

Bullfighting has been popular in Spain since the 1700s. A bullfight, known as a *corrida* in Spanish, lasts about 20 minutes. The bullfighter, called a matador, encourages the bull to charge at him. The matador wears a brightly colored uniform called a "suit of lights," and carries a red cape. As the bull charges, the matador moves his body so that the bull just misses him. A combination of bravery and graceful gestures marks the best matadors, who usually become rich and popular stars. Bulls are bred specially for bullfights.

THE BRITISH ISLES

The British Isles are made up of the United Kingdom (England, Scotland, Wales, and Northern Ireland) and Ireland. The islands are separated from mainland Europe by the English Channel.

England is the most densely populated part of the British Isles. Many people live in the industrial cities in the north of England and Midlands, or in the southeast, near London. Other parts of England are mainly rural. Mountains and lakes dominate the northwest. The southwest of England has a spectacular coastline of cliffs and bays, while the south and east are regions of gently sloping hills and rich farmland.

Northern Scotland has spectacular mountains and deep valleys, called glens. The central part of Scotland has fertile farmland and industrial centers. Farther south, hills provide excellent sheep grazing.

Wales is mountainous with deep river valleys. Most people live in the strip of flat land along the south coast. Oil refining, steel working, and sheep farming are important activities. Northern Ireland has low mountains and rich pastureland.

Ireland, separated from England, Scotland, and Wales by the Irish Sea, is mainly a farming country, but industry and tourism are also important.

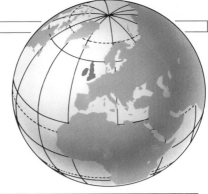

Below Tower Bridge crosses the River Thames next to the historic Tower of London. The road over the bridge is raised when ships pass underneath. Visitors can get a memorable view of London from the top of Tower Bridge.

Above Stone cottages nestle at the foot of the tallest Welsh mountains in Snowdonia National Park. The rural countryside and abundant rainfall provide excellent conditions for raising sheep, and Welsh lamb is famous around the world. The slate used on the roofs comes from mines worked locally.

Ruler of the land

The United Kingdom has a form of government called a constitutional monarchy. Government decisions are taken by Parliament, under the direction of the Prime Minister and the Cabinet. The monarchy approves these decisions and is responsible for affairs of state, such as representing the country at formal occasions at home and abroad. Queen Elizabeth II (right) is the reigning monarch. Prince Charles is the heir to the throne.

IRELAND/EIRE
Capital: Dublin
Population: 3,557,000

UNITED KINGDOM
Capital: London
Population: 57,121,000

Right Roman sentries once patrolled Hadrian's Wall, which runs from coast to coast across the bleak moors of northern England. It was built nearly 2,000 years ago to ward off frequent invaders from Scotland.

Above A kilted competitor tosses the caber, a heavy wooden pole, at the Highland Games. The games, held regularly in the Scottish Highlands, test competitors' skills and strength in a series of traditional events.

ATLANTIC OCEAN

ORKNEY IS.

Outer Hebrides

Inner Hebrides

Spey

▲ Ben Nevis

Grampians

• Aberdeen

SCOTLAND

Glasgow • • Edinburgh

NORTH SEA

NORTHERN IRELAND
Lough Neagh
• Belfast

IRELAND (Eire)

Shannon

ISLE OF MAN

IRISH SEA

□ Dublin

Lake District

Pennines

• Leeds

Manchester •

Snowdonia

Trent

WALES

Birmingham •

Swansea •

Cardiff •

ENGLAND

Severn

Bath •

London □

Thames

Southampton •

Plymouth •

ISLE OF WIGHT

ENGLISH CHANNEL

Riddle of the ancient stones

The mysterious stone monument of Stonehenge is located about 8 miles (13 km) north of Salisbury in the West Country of England. Parts of it date back to 3100 BC, before the Pyramids were built in Egypt. Pairs of upright stones known as sarsens form the inner circle. They weigh 5 tons each, but had to be transported more than 18 miles (29 km) to build Stonehenge. The exact purpose of Stonehenge puzzles experts, but many believe that it had a religious function. On important days such as midsummer the sun rises directly behind certain stones of the outer circle.

Left A visitor to Blarney Castle in Ireland leans back to kiss the Blarney Stone in order to receive the stone's famous "gift of the gab."

miles
0   100
0   100
kilometers

FRANCE, BELGIUM, THE NETHERLANDS, AND LUXEMBOURG

These countries, which lie on the western edge of mainland Europe, are among Europe's richest and most developed. Belgium, the Netherlands, and Luxembourg are sometimes known as the Benelux countries.

France is the second largest country in Europe. The northern areas are flat, fertile farmland and contain much heavy industry. The high mountain ranges of the Alps and the Jura in the east and the Pyrenees in the southwest are thinly populated but are excellent for skiing and rambling. The beaches of the Riviera along the Mediterranean coast attract tourists. Large rivers run through the fertile fields and forests of the rest of the country. France has a prosperous agricultural industry, and French farmers produce some of the world's finest wines, cheeses, and produce.

The Netherlands and most of Belgium are very flat. More than 40 percent of the Netherlands has been reclaimed from the sea. Many agricultural and industrial goods are exported from Rotterdam. It is one of the busiest ports in the world.

Belgium is one of the world's most densely populated countries. The headquarters of the EC and North Atlantic Treaty Organization (NATO) are both situated in Brussels. Luxembourg is an important center of international banking.

Above Medieval buildings line the canals of Bruges, a Belgian city noted for its weaving and lace-making. Its inhabitants call it by its Flemish name, Brugge, which means "bridges."

Below Artists sell their work in Place du Tertre, in the Parisian district called Montmartre. Artists first made Montmartre their base in the 19th century, when it was a separate village.

Above Flowers are big business in the Netherlands. Tulips and daffodils make the fields blaze with color each spring. A row of poplar trees protects the field from gusts of wind.

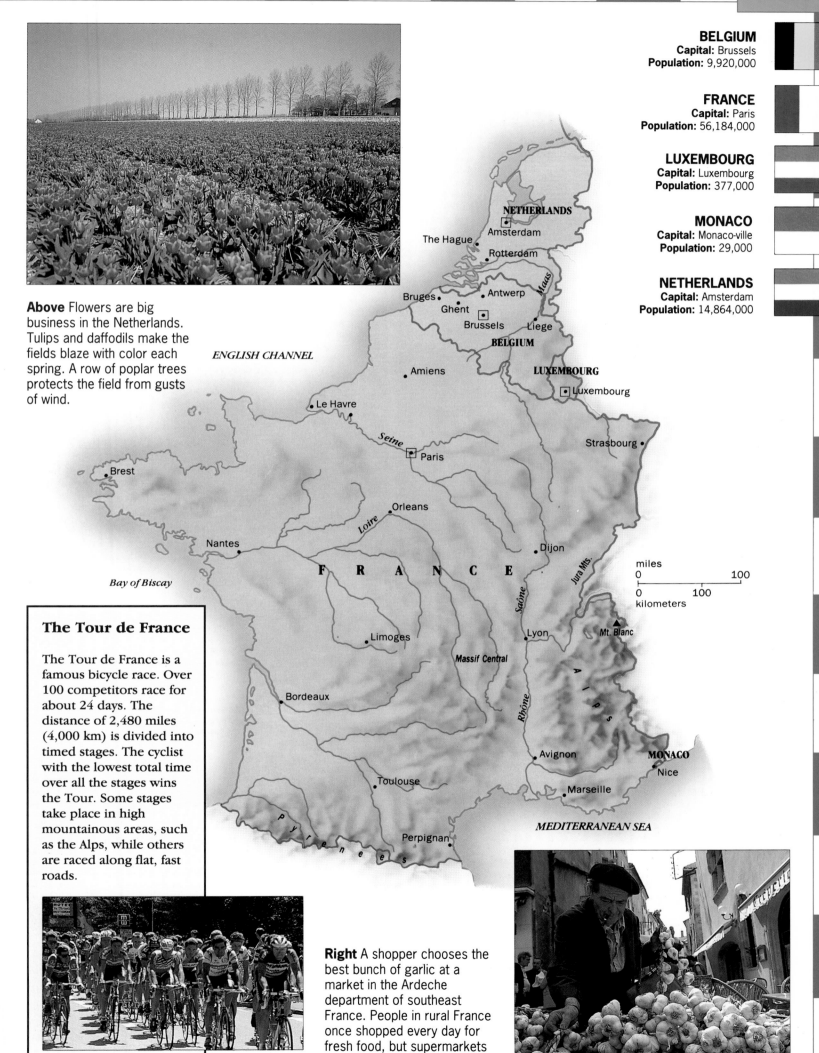

BELGIUM
Capital: Brussels
Population: 9,920,000

FRANCE
Capital: Paris
Population: 56,184,000

LUXEMBOURG
Capital: Luxembourg
Population: 377,000

MONACO
Capital: Monaco-ville
Population: 29,000

NETHERLANDS
Capital: Amsterdam
Population: 14,864,000

NETHERLANDS
Amsterdam
The Hague
Rotterdam
Bruges
Ghent
Antwerp
Brussels
Liege
BELGIUM
LUXEMBOURG
Luxembourg
Amiens
Strasbourg
Le Havre
Seine
Paris
Brest
Orleans
Loire
Nantes
Dijon
Jura Mts.
Limoges
Lyon
Mt. Blanc
Massif Central
Alps
Bordeaux
Rhône
Saône
Avignon
MONACO
Nice
Toulouse
Marseille
Perpignan
Pyrenees
F R A N C E
ENGLISH CHANNEL
Bay of Biscay
MEDITERRANEAN SEA
Maas

miles
0 — 100
0 — 100
kilometers

The Tour de France

The Tour de France is a famous bicycle race. Over 100 competitors race for about 24 days. The distance of 2,480 miles (4,000 km) is divided into timed stages. The cyclist with the lowest total time over all the stages wins the Tour. Some stages take place in high mountainous areas, such as the Alps, while others are raced along flat, fast roads.

Right A shopper chooses the best bunch of garlic at a market in the Ardeche department of southeast France. People in rural France once shopped every day for fresh food, but supermarkets are changing their habits.

GERMANY, AUSTRIA, AND SWITZERLAND

Germany is a rich and powerful country, selling manufactured goods worldwide. Its largest land region, the North German Plain, is low and flat. Large rivers, including the Elbe, Ems, Oder, Rhine, Ruhr, and Weser, are important commercial waterways linking this industrial and farming area.

Much of central Germany is mountainous and heavily forested. Wooded areas such as the Black Forest provide raw materials for the manufacture of paper. Fertile farmland is found in the South German hills.

Germany was divided into East and West from 1949 until 1990. The first all-German elections since 1937 were held in late 1990. Eastern Germany has many factories but the standard of living is still lower than in the rest of the country.

Austria and Switzerland are landlocked countries with spectacular mountain scenery. More than half of the Austrian population lives in cities, and over 20 percent lives in the capital, Vienna. Most of Switzerland's population lives on a central plateau between the Alps and the Jura mountains.

Both Austria and Switzerland produce high-precision industrial exports such as electrical goods, machinery, and wrist watches.

Gateway to the north

The Rhine River, which rises in the Swiss Alps, flows through Germany and the Netherlands before it flows out into the North Sea. It is about 820 miles (1,319 km) long. Many rivers, including the Mosel, flow into the Rhine, while others, such as the Rhone, are connected to it by canals. The Rhine is used as a main route for barges carrying heavy, bulky goods through Europe. The river flows through the Rhine valley, which is overlooked by many historic castles.

Right Outdoor cafes, smart boutiques, and department stores line the Kurfursten-damm, or "Ku-damm," Berlin's liveliest and most elegant thoroughfare. Behind is the shell of Kaiser Wilhelm Gedachtniskirche, a church that was nearly destroyed in World War II. It is now a war memorial.

Left Shoppers in the Rhine port of Mainz eye the goods at the market in the city's central square. The houses in the center of this old German city are a mixture of medieval and modern.

A driving force

Germany has one of the oldest and most important car-making industries in the world. The Germans have been manufacturing automobiles since 1889, when Gottlieb Daimler invented the first car to run on gasoline. Daimler-Benz, which was founded by the inventor, is now the largest company in Germany. Overall, the Germans produce more than 4.6 million cars each year. Only Japan and the United States produce more. About half of these cars are exported. German cars have a reputation for high quality, from the widely popular Volkswagen models to the more luxurious models such as Mercedes-Benz, BMW, and Audi.

AUSTRIA
Capital: Vienna
Population: 7,650,000

GERMANY
Capital: Bonn/Berlin
Population: 79,070,000

LIECHTENSTEIN
Capital: Vaduz
Population: 29,000

SWITZERLAND
Capital: Bern
Population: 6,628,000

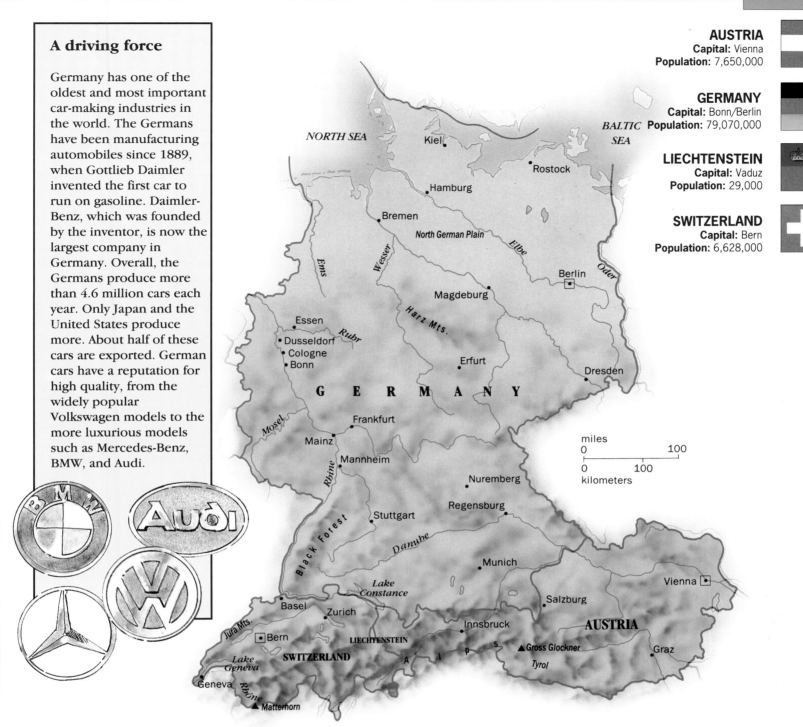

Left The colorful clothing of skiers stands out against the snowy background at Portes du Soleil, a popular ski resort in the French-speaking region of Switzerland.

Right The harplike notes of the zither are a familiar sound in the taverns and cafes of southern Germany and Austria. Zithers provide the musical accompaniment to the alpine folk songs and yodeling of Bavaria and the Austrian Tyrol.

POLAND AND CZECHOSLOVAKIA

Poland and Czechoslovakia lie in the eastern part of Europe. Czechoslovakia is landlocked, while Poland has a northern coastline along the Baltic Sea. The Western Carpathian Mountains in the south of Poland extend into Czechoslovakia. This forested wilderness includes some of Europe's most spectacular scenery as well as wild animals, including eagles, wild boar, and bears.

Most Poles live in the southeast of the country, in the Polish Uplands. This is the most industrialized part of the country. Coal, iron, and steel are produced. Until 1990, almost all of Polish industry was owned by the state. Now, most industry in the country is privately owned.

Warsaw, Poland's capital, is situated in the Central Plains, the country's main agricultural area. Poland is one of the world's leading producers of potatoes and rye. The Baltic coast has sandy beaches and the ports of Gdansk, Gdynia, and Szczecin.

Czechoslovakia has been industrialized for many years. Among the items Czechoslovakia produces are iron, steel, shoes, and textiles.

Roughly 40 percent of Czechoslovakia's population works in industry. Two thirds are Czechs, found mostly in Bohemia and Moravia, the industrialized areas in the west of the country. The remaining third are Slovaks, living in the more fertile eastern area known as Slovakia. Czechoslovakia is now divided into two separate republics, the Czech Republic and the Slovak Republic, each of which has its own government.

Left Pine forests border the rolling farmland in southern Poland. The rich soil of this region is the best in the country growing a wide range of crops, including sugar beet, wheat, potatoes, and rye.

Right Polish customs have remained strong despite centuries of rule by powerful neighbors. These children, dressed in traditional costumes, are taking part in a Polish folk dancing festival.

City of a hundred spires

Prague, the capital of Czechoslovakia, is one of Europe's oldest and most beautiful cities. It gets its nickname because of its many churches. Prague lies on the banks of the Vltava River which is spanned by a number of bridges. Charles Bridge (right) is popular with artists and sightseers in Prague.

Above A baroque church lies along the outer walls of Tabor, an important city in the Czech region of Bohemia. Behind the city walls is a maze of winding streets that were designed to confuse invaders.

CZECHOSLOVAKIA
Capital: Prague
Population: 15,695,000

POLAND
Capital: Warsaw
Population: 38,363,000

BALTIC SEA

Gdynia
Gdansk
Elblag
Szczecin

Poznan
Vistula
Central Plain
Warsaw
Bug

P O L A N D

Lublin

Wroclaw

Katowice
Krakow

Ore Mts.
MORAVIA
Sudeten Mts.
CZECH REPUBLIC
Ostrava
Carpathian Mts.
BOHEMIA
Prague
Brno
Vltava
C Z E C H O S L O V A K I A
Kosice
SLOVAK REPUBLIC
SLOVAKIA
Bratislava
Danube

miles
0   100
0   100
kilometers

Life through the looking glass

Filmmakers have tapped Czechoslovakia's traditions of mime and puppetry to develop a distinctive type of film animation. Their short animated films often highlight funny aspects of daily life. Using techniques such as silhouettes or plainly drawn images, these animators produce comic effects. Animated films in the 1960s and 1970s were less censored by the government than those using real actors and actresses. Many of Czechoslovakia's best animators were trained at that time.

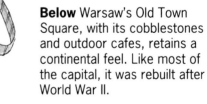

Left Gdansk is Poland's largest port. This view from the town hall shows the medieval heart of the city. For many years Gdansk was called Danzig.

Below Warsaw's Old Town Square, with its cobblestones and outdoor cafes, retains a continental feel. Like most of the capital, it was rebuilt after World War II.

HUNGARY, ROMANIA, AND BULGARIA

Hungary, Romania, and Bulgaria lie in eastern Europe. Romania and Bulgaria have ports on the Black Sea, but Hungary is landlocked. All three are developing as industrial nations. Private companies are replacing the state-owned firms that dominated the economies in all three countries.

Fertile plains cover most of Hungary. Balaton, one of Europe's largest lakes, lies in the west of the country. Hungarian farmers produce a wide variety of fruits and grains, some of which they export, along with large quantities of paprika, which flavors the fiery national dish, goulash. The wine-producing industry is flourishing.

Spectacular wooded mountains cover most of Romania and Bulgaria. These mountains provide timber and minerals. Romania also has large deposits of oil and natural gas. Farming is also important in Bulgaria, although only 38 percent of the land can be used for crops. Bulgaria exports grains, tomatoes, sugar beet, and wine.

Hungary, Romania, and Bulgaria are linked to the rest of Europe and to the Black Sea by the mighty Danube River, into which most of the countries' other rivers flow. The Danube serves as an important transportation route for the countries' industries, with many boats plying up and down the river.

Below The Council Tower in the Romanian town of Sibiu was built in 1588. Sibiu, a centuries-old trading center, lies on Romania's central plain, in the region of Transylvania. The Carpathian Alps rise up south of Sibiu.

Land of roses

One of Bulgaria's most valuable exports is rose oil, a thick, sweet-smelling liquid made by distilling rose blossoms and petals. Rose oil is used in perfumes and as a food flavoring. Most rose oil comes from the Vale of Roses at the foot of the Stara Planina, a mountain range in northern Bulgaria.

Bridging the Danube

Budapest, the capital of Hungary, on the banks of the Danube River, was once three separate cities – Buda, Pest, and Obuda. In 1873, these cities joined with Margaret Island in the Danube, to form Budapest. The west bank of the river (the original Buda) contains many beautiful buildings. Eight bridges across the Danube link Buda with what used to be Pest, on the east bank. Here are many government offices, the Parliament building, and Budapest's industrial areas. Many of Budapest's buildings were destroyed during World War II and have since been rebuilt in their original style. About 20 percent of Hungary's population lives in the city.

Right Two Romanian farmers use a horse-cart to transport their hay. Romania's way of life has undergone many changes in the last 50 years, with many villages destroyed to make way for new towns and cities. But those peasants who remained on farms use methods that have hardly changed for centuries.

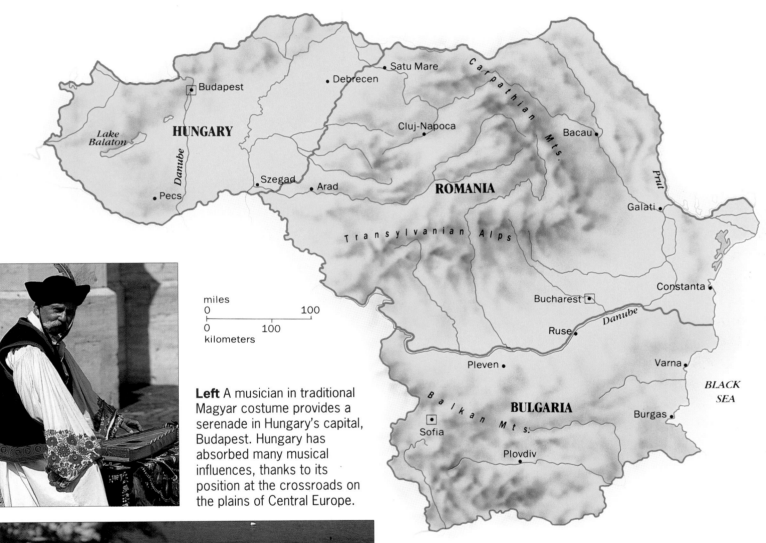

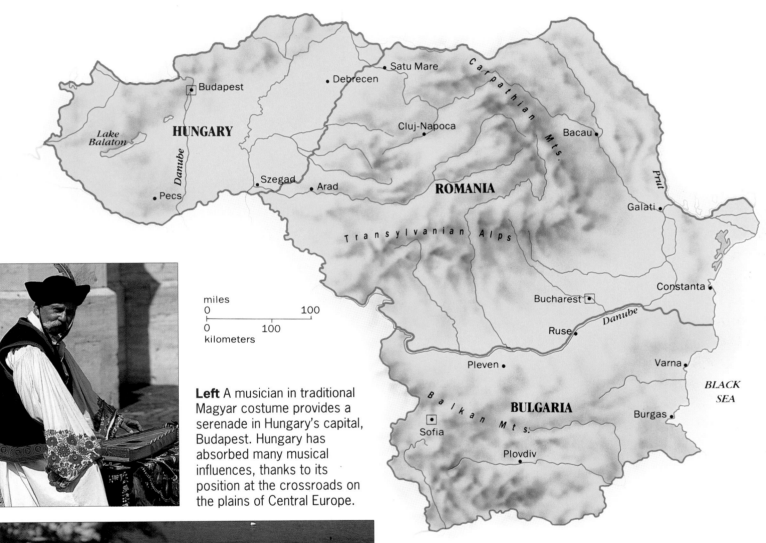

BULGARIA
Capital: Sofia
Population: 8,978,000

HUNGARY
Capital: Budapest
Population: 10,546,000

ROMANIA
Capital: Bucharest
Population: 23,269,000

Left A musician in traditional Magyar costume provides a serenade in Hungary's capital, Budapest. Hungary has absorbed many musical influences, thanks to its position at the crossroads on the plains of Central Europe.

Left The mild climate and long, sandy beaches of Bulgaria's Black Sea coast make it a popular holiday destination for Bulgarians and other East Europeans. This resort is called Golden Sands.

Right The waters of the Black Sea contain herring, mackerel, pike, perch, and bream, which the Bulgarians catch using small boats and simple fishing methods.

Map labels: Satu Mare, Budapest, Debrecen, Cluj-Napoca, Bacau, Lake Balaton, HUNGARY, Danube, Carpathian Mts., Prut, Szegad, Arad, ROMANIA, Galati, Pecs, Transylvanian Alps, Constanta, Bucharest, Danube, Ruse, Pleven, Varna, BLACK SEA, Balkan Mts., BULGARIA, Burgas, Sofia, Plovdiv

miles
0 ——— 100
0 ——— 100
kilometers

ITALY AND SOUTHEASTERN EUROPE

Italy and the republics of Yugoslavia, Greece, and Albania lie along the Mediterranean Sea in southeastern Europe. They are mainly mountainous, with some fertile valleys and uplands. Their Mediterranean climate, with hot summers and cool, wet winters, favors crops such as olives, citrus fruits, and grapes.

Italy's boot-shaped peninsula stands out on any map of Europe. The Appenine Mountains run down the center of this peninsula. Vatican City and San Marino, two of the world's smallest countries, are surrounded by Italian territory. Malta, which is also independent, lies south of Sicily.

Italy is one of the most prosperous countries in Europe. Italian products combine usefulness with a lively sense of style. The Italians are famous for their well-designed cars, household goods, shoes, and clothing. Most industry is concentrated around the northern cities of Milan, Turin, and Genoa. Farming is widespread, and fruit and vegetables are grown in every region. Italy leads the world in wine production.

Yugoslavia is a mixture of Alpine meadows, bare stone mountains, and fertile valleys. Since 1991 four of its six republics have declared independence, reflecting the aspirations of the Serbs, Croats, Slovenes, Bosnians, and other nationalities living there.

Mountains run through nearly every part of Greece, which has more than 2,000 islands. Industry and trade are concentrated in the main cities of Athens and Thessaloniki. Coastal areas rely on tourism and fishing to maintain their economies.

Albania was a mystery for decades until it opened its doors to the outside world in the late 1980s. Mountains cover most of the country. Albania's mainly rural population is concentrated in two main farming areas, along the Adriatic Sea, and in the fertile Koritza Basin, where wheat, corn, sugar beet, potatoes, and fruit are grown.

Vatican City

The Vatican City is the smallest independent state in the world. The City is situated in Rome, and it is the headquarters of the Roman Catholic Church as ruled by the Pope. The Pope lives in the Vatican Palace. The Vatican City has its own car license plates.

Above An intricate network of canals links every part of the Italian city of Venice. Boats, called gondolas, transport local residents, tourists, and even cargo through Venice. The city is built on a number of islands in a lagoon off the coast of northeastern Italy. Water is the most important feature of Venice, which risks severe floods after heavy rain.

CROATIA
Capital: Zagreb
Population: 4,547,000

MACEDONIA
Capital: Skopje
Population: 1,925,000

SLOVENIA
Capital: Ljubljana
Population: 1,919,000

YUGOSLAVIA
Capital: Belgrade
Population: 10,000,000

BOSNIA-HERZEGOVINA
Capital: Sarajevo
Population: 4,173,000

ALBANIA
Capital: Tirana
Population: 3,268,000

GREECE
Capital: Athens
Population: 10,066,000

ITALY
Capital: Rome
Population: 57,657,000

MALTA
Capital: Valletta
Population: 354,900

SAN MARINO
Capital: San Marino
Population: 23,000

VATICAN CITY
Capital: Vatican City
Population: 750

Olympic fire

The first Olympic Games took place at Olympia in Greece in 776 BC. In 1896 the Games were revived in Athens. The new Olympic Games open with a parade of athletes, during which the Olympic flame, a flaming torch on a tall stand, is lit by a smaller torch that has been carried from the Valley of Olympia by runners.

Below Boys play in a field in Zerqani, a farming settlement in central Albania. Farmers in this mountainous region have very little machinery and can farm only on small plots.

Below Whitewashed houses give a bright look to Thira, the capital of the Greek island of Santorini. It is built on the edge of a crater formed by a volcanic eruption in 1450 BC.

SCANDINAVIA, FINLAND, AND ICELAND

Scandinavia is the name used to refer to Norway, Sweden, and Denmark. Along with Finland, these countries lie in the north of Europe. Iceland is an island situated in the North Atlantic Ocean off the east coast of Greenland. Despite their small populations, these five countries are among the wealthiest in the world.

Parts of Norway, Sweden, and Finland extend well beyond the Arctic Circle, so their populations are concentrated in the warmer south where the land is more fertile. Narrow, mountainous harbors, called fjords, are a feature of Norway's coastline, while the Swedish and Finnish countryside is flatter, with forests and hundreds of lakes.

Paper and wood account for over 40 percent of Finland's exports and about one quarter of Sweden's. These two countries also have successful engineering industries. Fishing and North Sea oil drilling are the chief sources of Norway's wealth.

Denmark consists of a peninsula, Jutland, and 482 islands. Over half the population lives on the islands. Denmark produces goods such as machinery, textiles, porcelains, and silverware, as well as foods such as bacon and dairy products.

The central part of Iceland is a rugged, barren area famous for its volcanoes, hot springs, geysers, and glaciers.

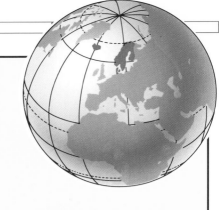

The Midnight Sun

The "Midnight Sun" describes a six-month period when the sun is up 24 hours a day. This happens only in the Earth's polar regions. At the North Pole, the sun never sets from March 20 to September 23. Then there are six months of darkness. The northern areas of Norway, Sweden, and Finland lie within the Arctic Circle and are called the "Land of the Midnight Sun."

Above Sheer cliffs line the sides of the narrow bays, called fjords, along Norway's Atlantic coast. Some fjords are more than 4,000 ft (1,200 m) deep, allowing freighters and cruise ships to sail through the narrow passages.

Left Logs are floated for collection and processing along the Kemi River in northern Finland. The logging industry uses more than 25,000 miles (40,000 km) of waterways to transport logs each spring.

Outlying islands

ICELAND

Reykjavik

Vatnajokull Glacier

ATLANTIC OCEAN

Iceland (left) is an island country in the north Atlantic, about 500 miles (800 km) west of Norway. This location, nearly at the Arctic Circle, means that Reykjavik is the world's most northerly capital. The Icelandic language is similar to the one spoken by the Vikings. The Faroe Islands (right) lie 300 miles (480 km) southeast of Iceland. They are part of Denmark but are self-governing in most matters.

FAROE IS. (DENMARK)

DENMARK
Capital: Copenhagen
Population: 5,134,000

FINLAND
Capital: Helsinki
Population: 4,977,000

ICELAND
Capital: Reykjavik
Population: 251,000

NORWAY
Capital: Oslo
Population: 4,214,000

SWEDEN
Capital: Stockholm
Population: 8,407,000

Above Lapp children in traditional clothing prepare to harness a reindeer to a sleigh in Finland. Herds of reindeer also provide the Lapps with meat, skins, and dairy products.

North Cape

NORWEGIAN SEA

Tromso

Lapland

Lake Inari

LOFOTEN IS

Narvik

Muonio

Kemi

Lule

Ume

Lake Oulu

FINLAND

Gulf of Bothnia

Trondheim

ATLANTIC OCEAN

Sognefjord

Bergen

NORWAY

Hardanger Plateau

Oslo

Stavanger

SWEDEN

Tampere

Lake Päijanne

Turku

Helsinki

Uppsala

ALAND IS.

Vasteras

Stockholm

Lake Vanern

Norrkoping

Lake Vattern

Skagerrak

Goteborg

GOTLAND

NORTH SEA

Jutland

Herning   Copenhagen   Helsingborg

BALTIC SEA

DENMARK

Malmo

Odense

BORNHOLM

miles
0   250

0   250
kilometers

Raiders from the north

The Vikings lived in Scandinavia over 1,000 years ago. Viking raiders attacked parts of Europe. They came in strong boats called longships. The crew rowed and sailed the ship, then fought on land with axes and swords. The Vikings were great navigators who sailed to and settled in places as far away as Greenland and Iceland. Historians now believe Vikings may have sailed as far as America.

Right Brightly colored boathouses line the shores of Vattern, one of the largest lakes in Sweden. Many Swedes have lakeside holiday homes.

THE RUSSIAN FEDERATION AND EASTERN EUROPE

The vast area of land on the eastern edge of Europe used to be known as the Union of Soviet Socialist Republics, or the USSR. The Russian Federation, the Baltic States, Belarus, Ukraine, Moldova, and Georgia were all part of the USSR, but are now independent republics. Most now belong to a loose grouping called the Commonwealth of Independent States.

The Russian Federation, made up of 16 separate republics, extends from the Baltic Sea to the North Pacific. Most Russians live in the west, in the area known as the European Plains. Here, there is rich soil for farming and great open grasslands called steppes. Stretching down through the center of Russia are the Ural Mountains, which have massive mineral deposits.

Estonia, Latvia, and Lithuania are the Baltic States. They lie on a coastal plain, with low-lying farmland, hills, lakes, and swamps.

Belarus and Ukraine lie on Russia's southwestern border. Much of Belarus is marshy, but almost a quarter of the country is forest. Ukraine and Moldova have rich farmland. Georgia lies on Russia's mountainous southern boundary. Vines, tea, and tobacco are grown on steep hillsides. Georgia has large deposits of manganese, coal, and oil.

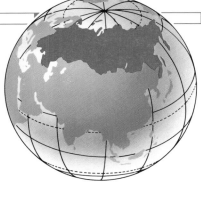

Left The exotic domes and colorful architecture of St. Basil's Cathedral make it one of Russia's most famous landmarks. It stands at one end of Red Square in Moscow.

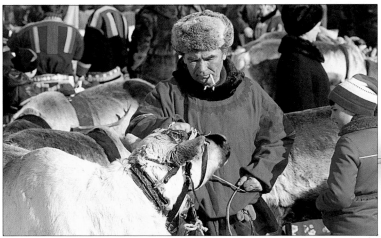

Above The Russian people have learned to adapt to their bitterly cold climate and have developed a wide range of winter sports. This man is preparing his team of deer for a sleigh race near Murmansk, in northern Russia.

Below Moscow Circus dancers in Asian costume captivate the audience with their elaborate choreography. The Circus, which occasionally tours the world, is also famous for its daring acrobatics and its popular clowns.

BARENTS SEA

• Murmansk

Arkhangelsk

Lake Ladoga   Lake Onega

St. Petersburg

Tallinn   Nizhny Novgorod

ESTONIA

LATVIA Riga   Moscow

LITHUANIA   Kanz

Vilnius   Minsk

BELARUS

Kiev   Kharkov

Kishinev   **UKRAINE** • Donetsk

MOLDOVA   Odessa   Caucasus Mts.

BLACK SEA

Tbilisi

GEORGIA

The price of freedom

A network of indoor arcades runs through GUM, a large shopping center in the heart of Moscow. Until the end of 1991 the government controlled the supply and prices of goods. Shoppers faced price increases when controls were lifted in 1992.

Answered prayers

The Orthodox Church is the traditional religion of most Russians. For many years religious services were discouraged by the government. Many churches were closed, or converted for other purposes. These controls ended in the 1980s. Churches reopened, and many people returned to their traditional faith.

Right A Hakka horseman returns to the family tent in Siberia. The Hakka are a Chinese people who have lived on the Siberian steppes and tundra for centuries. Traditionally they were nomadic, earning their living as livestock raisers and moving their tents to follow their herds. Russian influence over the last 100 years has led many of the Hakka to settle on farms.

BELARUS
Capital: Minsk
Population: 10,200,000

ESTONIA
Capital: Tallinn
Population: 1,600,000

GEORGIA
Capital: Tbilisi
Population: 5,500,000

LATVIA
Capital: Riga
Population: 2,700,000

LITHUANIA
Capital: Vilnius
Population: 3,700,000

MOLDOVA
Capital: Kishinev
Population: 4,300,000

RUSSIA
Capital: Moscow
Population: 147,000,000

UKRAINE
Capital: Kiev
Population: 51,700,000

Map labels:

ARCTIC OCEAN
SEVERNAYA ZEMLYA
NEW SIBERIAN ISLANDS
LAPTEV SEA
NOVAYA ZEMLYA
KARA SEA
EAST SIBERIAN SEA
WRANGEL I.
Verkhoyansk Range
Central Siberian Plateau
Kolyma Mts.
BERING SEA
West Siberian Plain
Yenisey
Lena
Ural Mts.
Ob
RUSSIAN FEDERATION
Magadan
Kamchatka Peninsula
erm
Chelyabinsk
Omsk
Novosibirsk
Lake Baykal
Irkutsk
Chita
Stanovoy Range
SEA OF OKHOTSK
nara
Sayan Mts.
Amur
SAKHALIN
Altai Mts.
Vladivostok

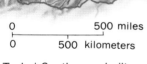

0   500 miles
0   500 kilometers

Below Trakei Castle was built in the Middle Ages, when Lithuania and the other Baltic states faced invasions from Russia and from the countries of western Europe.

Below Swimmers enjoy the sunshine and warm Black Sea waters at Sukhumi, a resort on Georgia's coast. The sea air and southern latitude of Sukhumi give it a climate like that of many Mediterranean beaches.

SECTION 3: ASIA

More than half of the world's population lives in Asia, where age-old traditions survive in the face of the newest high technology. Farmers with ox-drawn plows work fields in the shadow of skyscrapers and factories producing computers and video games.

INTRODUCTION

The 47 countries of Asia cover a vast area, almost one third of the Earth's total land area, while its population accounts for about three fifths of the world's people.

Asia is divided into five main regions. In the west is the Middle East, while in the north and center lie the Central Asian Republics, which were once part of the USSR. East Asia includes China, Japan, and Korea. India and Pakistan are the largest countries in the south of the continent, while the countries to the east and south of India form the region known as Southeast Asia.

The northernmost parts of Asia experience bitterly cold winters, while the southernmost parts lie in the hot, steamy tropical areas around the Equator. Asia has towering mountain ranges and arid deserts as well as vast inland lakes and seas. The world's highest mountain, Mount Everest, rises to a height of 29,088 feet (8,863 m) in the Himalayas, while the Dead Sea, the lowest place on earth at 1,313 feet (400 m) below sea level, lies in Jordan.

Farmers make up 60 percent of Asia's population, but over-population means that there are often shortages. Natural disasters such as typhoons and floods also cause famine, devastation, and great loss of life.

Some Asian countries, such as Japan, South Korea, Taiwan, and Singapore, have highly developed industries. They are world leaders in many areas of high-technology manufacturing. The Middle East produces a large proportion of the world's oil, and more than half the world's tin.

Above Japanese schoolchildren assemble during an outing in Tokyo. Discipline and hard work are stressed in Japanese schools.

Left A traditional thatch-roofed farmhouse sits beneath a cliff in Guizhou, China. More than two thirds of China's population live on farms.

Right Yemen is a remote, mountainous country in the south of the Arabian peninsula. In biblical times it was ruled by the Queen of Sheba.

Left A terraced farm clings to the Himalayan foothills in Nepal. The Nepalese and other mountain people use terraces to collect rainwater and to create more space to cultivate.

Below The golden tower of Swedagon Pagoda looms over the Burmese capital, Rangoon. Burma's Buddhist traditions go back more than 2,000 years.

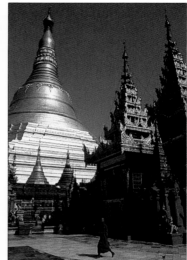

THE COUNTRIES OF ASIA

36
Armenia, Azerbaijan, Kazakhstan, Kyrgyzstan, Tajikistan, Turkmenistan, Uzbekistan

38
China, Hong Kong, Macau, Mongolia

40
Japan, North Korea, South Korea, Taiwan

42
Afghanistan, Bangladesh, Bhutan, India, Nepal, Maldives, Pakistan, Sri Lanka

44
Brunei, Burma, Cambodia, Indonesia, Laos, Malaysia, Philippines, Singapore, Thailand, Vietnam

46
Bahrain, Iran, Iraq, Israel, Jordan, Kuwait, Lebanon, Oman, Qatar, Saudi Arabia, Syria, Turkey, United Arab Emirates, Yemen

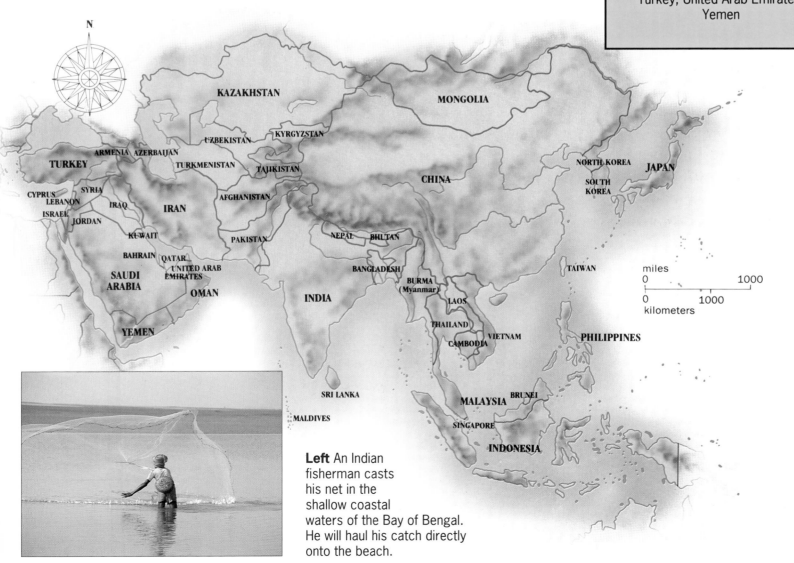

Left An Indian fisherman casts his net in the shallow coastal waters of the Bay of Bengal. He will haul his catch directly onto the beach.

Rich pickings from the sea

Caviar is one of the world's most expensive delicacies. People associate it with champagne and the dinner parties of the very rich. It is simply the roe (eggs) of sturgeon or beluga, a special type of white sturgeon. Caviar can be either red or black, depending on the type of fish that laid the eggs. Most of the caviar in the former Soviet Union comes from the waters of the Caspian Sea, which is like a large inland, salt-water lake. High-quality caviar has become even more expensive in recent years. This is partly because of overfishing.

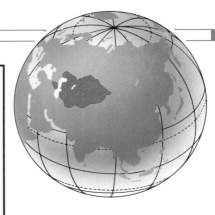

Below The Aral Sea is a large lake, on the border between Kazakhstan and Uzbekistan. It has nearly dried up due to the irrigation of the deserts.

CENTRAL ASIAN REPUBLICS

The seven Central Asian Republics occupy an area between two mountain ranges: the Caucasus in the west and the Pamirs in the southeast. The area includes the Caspian Sea, as well as the deserts of Kara Kum and Kyzyl Kum. Many nationalities, including Armenians, Azerbaijanis, Uzbeks, and Turkomans, live in this region. Some of the languages spoken are related to Turkish or to Farsi, the language spoken in Iran. New ties with these two countries have been established since the former Soviet Union disbanded.

Armenia and Azerbaijan are largely rugged and mountainous, but fruit and cotton are grown in the low-lying areas. Armenia has large deposits of minerals, and Azerbaijan is rich in oil and natural gas.

The republics of Turkmenistan, Uzbekistan, and Kazakhstan consist mainly of grassy plateaus and sandy desert. Many of the people are nomadic and live by herding animals. Farming can only be done with the help of irrigation systems, but some fertile land lies along the Oxus River. Kazakhstan and Uzbekistan have valuable deposits of minerals, natural gas, and oil.

In the southeast lie the republics of Tajikistan and Kyrgyzstan. They are dominated by the Pamir Mountains, along the Chinese border. The land is barren, although the rocks are rich in minerals. Some mountain villagers breed yaks.

Above Turkmens belong to a group of Turkish people living in Central Asia. These Turkmens are wearing the *chugurmah*, a traditional head-dress made from the fur of the Karakul, a breed of sheep.

Right Samarkand is a center of Islamic learning in Uzbekistan. It was already a thriving city when Alexander the Great captured it in 329 BC. In the 14th century it was the capital of the Tartar empire.

Above The girls of the "Ulibka" dance ensemble perform some of the dance routines that are traditional in Kazakhstan.

Below Women gather for an outdoor meal that they have jointly prepared in Tashkent, capital of Uzbekistan. Traditions of hospitality are important to the people of Central Asia.

Below In many parts of Central Asia bread is still baked in traditional outdoor ovens, such as this one near Tashkent in Uzbekistan.

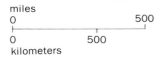

miles
0 _____ 500
0 _____ 500
kilometers

HONG KONG, CHINA, MONGOLIA, AND MACAU

China is the most heavily populated country in the world. Most Chinese live on farms in the eastern third of the country, where the mighty Yangtze Kiang River irrigates the fertile soil. Nearly all of China's major industrial cities, such as Shanghai and Beijing, are situated here, too. Although cities have huge populations and well-developed industries, most people live and work in the countryside. The combination of good soil, ample water, and a largely farming population enables China to produce almost all of its food needs.

The north and west of China are dominated by rugged mountains and vast deserts such as the Gobi Desert, which extends into Mongolia along China's northern border. Plateaus and towering mountain ranges cover much of Mongolia. Livestock is raised by most of the population, and animal products account for most of Mongolia's exports. Some Mongolians still live a nomadic life-style, while others have permanent homes.

Hong Kong and Macau lie on the southeastern tip of China. Hong Kong's land area is made up of a peninsula on mainland China, and over 235 islands. It will become part of China in 1997. Macau consists of a peninsula as well as the two islands of Coloane and Taipa.

Below The Great Wall of China extends 2,000 miles (3,220 km) across northern China. This system of walls and forts was built around 200 BC as a defense. It is so long that it can be seen from the moon.

Controlling the millions

China's population of more than 1.1 billion is the largest in the world. Chinese leaders recognize the problems of trying to ensure adequate food and living conditions for this growing population. Improved health conditions in China in recent decades mean that the birth rate far exceeds the death rate. Widespread health awareness campaigns and a better supply of medicines have encouraged this development. Family planning is a way to control the country's population explosion. The "China Plus One" program encourages married couples to have only one child. Experts predict that this policy will bring about a decline in China's population early in the next century.

Left Finding space to park a bicycle can be difficult in Beijing, China's capital. Bicycles are China's most common form of transportation, and very few people have cars. For every privately owned car in China, it is estimated that there are more than 400 bicycles.

CHINA
Capital: Beijing
Population: 1,130,065,000

HONG KONG
Capital: Victoria
Population: 5,900,000

MONGOLIA
Capital: Ulan Bator
Population: 2,185,000

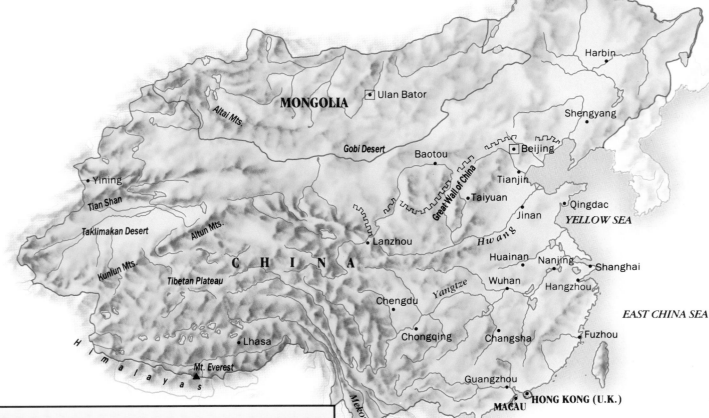

MONGOLIA
Ulan Bator
Harbin
Shengyang
Altai Mts.
Gobi Desert
Baotou
Beijing
Yining
Tianjin
Tian Shan
Great Wall of China
Taiyuan
Qingdac
Jinan
YELLOW SEA
Taklimakan Desert
Altun Mts.
Lanzhou
Hwang
C H I N A
Huainan
Nanjing
Shanghai
Kunlun Mts.
Wuhan
Hangzhou
Tibetan Plateau
Chengdu
Yangtze
EAST CHINA SEA
Himalayas
Lhasa
Chongqing
Changsha
Fuzhou
Mt. Everest
Guangzhou
Mekong
MACAU
HONG KONG (U.K.)
HAINAN I.
SOUTH CHINA SEA

miles
0   1000
0   1000
kilometers

Valuable junks

Junks are wooden sailing vessels that have been used in China for hundreds of years. Water transportation is widely used in China, as the country is crisscrossed by rivers and lakes that have been linked by a network of canals. The Grand Canal stretches for 1,106 miles (1,780 km) from Hangzhou to Beijing. Junks are able to carry heavy goods and can sail in shallow waters.

The commercial colony

Hong Kong is a British colony at the mouth of the Canton River in southern China. Hong Kong is a thriving industrial and trading center, and exports about 90 percent of its products. China will gain control of Hong Kong in 1997, but has promised to preserve its western-style economy.

JAPAN, TAIWAN, AND KOREA

Japan, Taiwan, and Korea lie in the eastern corner of Asia. They all have well-developed industries despite lacking raw materials.

Japan consists of four large islands and many smaller ones. Towering volcanic peaks and rocky gorges provide spectacular scenery, but force the majority of the population to live on the narrow plains along the coasts. Only 15 percent of Japan can be farmed but the land produces 70 percent of the food needed by the people.

Trade and industry have helped Japan develop one of the strongest economies in the world. The Japanese lead the world in car manufacturing, and set the pace in many high-technology industries such as micro-electronics. These manufacturers are concentrated along a southern coastal strip of Honshu, the largest island. Japan also has the largest fishing fleet in the world.

Thickly forested mountains cover the eastern half of the island of Taiwan. The west has gently rolling hills and fertile farmland. Taiwan's population is Chinese. The economy depends heavily on manufacturing.

Korea consists of a peninsula and over 3,000 islands, divided between the Democratic People's Republic of Korea (North Korea) and the Republic of Korea (South Korea). North Koreans work the land while the South Koreans depend more on manufacturing industries.

Below Fishing boats line the harbor of Suao, a port located about 30 miles (50 km) south of Taiwan's capital, Taipei. Taiwan is an important manufacturing country, but it also has a thriving food-processing industry.

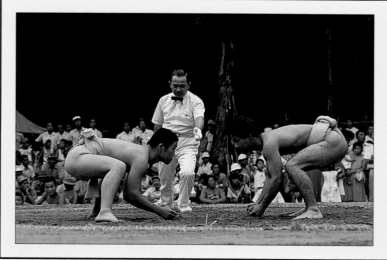

Heavyweight sport

Sumo is an ancient style of wrestling thought to have originated in Japan nearly 2,000 years ago. The wrestling takes place in a raised clay circle. A wrestler loses a match if any part of his body, except for the soles of his feet, touches the ground or if he steps or is pushed out of the ring by his opponent. There are many ancient ceremonies associated with sumo. It is very popular in Japan and successful wrestlers become as famous as pop stars. Wrestlers spend their whole time training to fight. They eat huge amounts of food to help them put on weight!

Steeped in tradition

The Japanese try to bring moments of peace and harmony to daily life. The tea ceremony has been a way of entertaining for more than 500 years. A host ushers guests into a special room where they are offered sweets. They can admire the tea set and decorations while the small kettle warms on a sunken fireplace, or *ro*. The host and guests continue their relaxed conversation over tea, knowing that personal or business matters will not be mentioned.

Above Japanese culture places great importance on the beauties of nature. Seasonal events, such as this cherry blossom festival in Tokyo, are popular family occasions.

JAPAN
Capital: Tokyo
Population: 123,778,000

NORTH KOREA
Capital: Pyongyang
Population: 23,059,000

SOUTH KOREA
Capital: Seoul
Population: 43,919,000

TAIWAN
Capital: Taipei
Population: 20,454,000

High-tech future

The strong Japanese economy is driven by the success of its high-technology manufacturers, including the computer, television, and other micro-electronics industries. The Japanese are on the forefront of new industrial techniques, such as specialized work teams and automation. They also invest heavily in research and development to keep ahead of the competition. Japanese engineers are now said to be designing a "new generation" of computers, that will be able to think for themselves.

Below Fish is a mainstay of the Korean diet, and the fishing fleets catch large numbers of cod, mackerel, crabs, and shrimp. These young South Korean boys have landed their own small catch from a local river.

Chongin

SEA OF JAPAN

JAPAN

Tokyo
Mt. Fuji ▲ Yokohama
Nagoya

NORTH KOREA

Pyongyang

Seoul   SOUTH KOREA

Inchon

Taegu

Pusan

Kyoto
Kobe   Osaka

HONSHU

Kitakyushu

SHIKOKU

Fukuoka

KYUSHU

Sapporo

HOKKAIDO

YELLOW SEA

PACIFIC OCEAN

EAST CHINA SEA

RYUKYU ISLANDS

miles
0   250

0   250
kilometers

Taipei

TAIWAN

Left Kirghiz nomads in northern Afghanistan shake out their handwoven rugs. Many people in remote parts of Afghanistan have been unaffected by the changes of the last two centuries.

Below Festive banners adorn a dusty street in rural Pakistan. Islamic celebrations and holy days are particularly important in Pakistan, where 97 percent of the population is Muslim.

BANGLADESH, INDIA, NEPAL, PAKISTAN, SRI LANKA, BHUTAN, AND AFGHANISTAN

The Indian subcontinent is bordered in the north by the Himalayas and in the south by the Indian Ocean. The region contains deserts, rain forests, huge plains, giant rivers, and high mountains.

India is the largest country in the sub-continent. Its people speak 16 different languages and over 1,000 dialects. About two thirds of them live on farms, but more than 250 million Indians are packed into crowded cities and towns. They work in industries ranging from large-scale manufacturing such as steel making to small family concerns such as carpet weaving. The small mountainous countries of Nepal and Bhutan lie on India's northeast border.

Many of Pakistan's people are farmers, living in the fertile plain of the Punjab. Pakistan also has important industries which process agricultural products, and produce cement, chemicals, and medicine. Most people who live in the barren Thar Desert and central and southern Afghanistan are

herders. Afghanistan has large, undeveloped mineral deposits locked in its mountains.

Bangladesh is a poor country, because it is impossible to grow enough food to feed the many people. The soil is rich by the mouth of the Ganges, but Bangladesh is often hit by natural disasters such as cyclones and floods.

Sri Lanka is an island. The population belongs to several racial groups, including Sinhalese and Tamils. Most of the people of Sri Lanka are farmers.

Roof of the world

The world's highest mountains are in the Himalayas, the mountain range called the "roof of the world." The tallest single mountain in the world, Mount Everest, is almost twice as high as Mont Blanc, Europe's tallest peak.

Mountain heights (chart):
- 30,250ft (9,000m)
- 26,800ft (8,000m) — Everest
- 23,450ft (7,000m) — Aconcagua
- 20,100ft (6,000m) — McKinley
- 16,750ft (5,000m) — Kilimanjaro, Vinson
- 13,400ft (4,000m) — Jaya, Mt Blanc
- 10,050ft (3,000m) — Cook
- 6,700ft (2,000m)
- 3,350ft (1,000m)
- 0

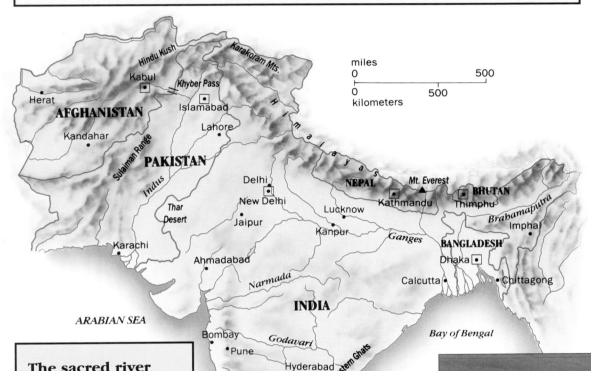

Map labels: Hindu Kush, Karakoram Mts., Kabul, Khyber Pass, Herat, AFGHANISTAN, Islamabad, Kandahar, Sulaiman Range, Lahore, PAKISTAN, Indus, Himalayas, Delhi, New Delhi, Thar Desert, Jaipur, Lucknow, Kanpur, NEPAL, Kathmandu, Mt. Everest, Thimphu, BHUTAN, Brahmaputra, Imphal, Ganges, BANGLADESH, Dhaka, Ahmadabad, Narmada, Calcutta, Chittagong, INDIA, ARABIAN SEA, Bay of Bengal, Bombay, Godavari, Pune, Hyderabad, Eastern Ghats, Western Ghats, Deccan Plateau, Bangalore, Madras, MALDIVES, SRI LANKA, Colombo, INDIAN OCEAN, Karachi

miles 0 — 500
kilometers 0 — 500

AFGHANISTAN
Capital: Kabul
Population: 15,592,000

BANGLADESH
Capital: Dhaka
Population: 107,992,000

BHUTAN
Capital: Thimphu
Population: 1,566,000

INDIA
Capital: New Delhi
Population: 844,000,000

MALDIVES
Capital: Malé
Population: 219,000

NEPAL
Capital: Kathmandu
Population: 19,158,000

PAKISTAN
Capital: Islamabad
Population: 113,163,000

SRI LANKA
Capital: Colombo
Population: 17,135,000

Below Benares is a holy city for India's millions of Hindus. They come to worship in its temples and bathe in the waters of the Ganges River.

The sacred river

The Ganges River flows for 1,802 miles (2,900 km) from its source in the Himalayas, through Bangladesh and into the Bay of Bengal. Hindus believe the Ganges to be a sacred river. Pilgrims visit holy cities such as Varanasi and Allahabad, which lie on the banks of the Ganges, to cleanse and purify themselves. Sick people come hoping for a cure, while others come to die in the river, believing that they will then be carried to Paradise.

Left People who live in India have traditionally created beautiful handmade rugs. The rugs are valuable because they have intricate designs and take a long time to make. Some rugs are woven on simple looms in village homes. Larger rugs may be made by several weavers working in a small factory. Most rugs are made of wool, but some of the most expensive rugs are made of silk.

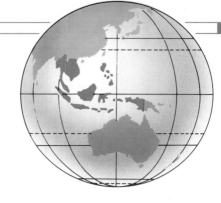

SOUTHEAST ASIA

The countries of Southeast Asia lie on a huge peninsula and on thousands of islands. Monsoons provide plenty of water and sunshine for the large areas of fertile soil.

Most people in Southeast Asia live in villages, and work on farms using traditional farming methods. The most important food crop is rice, but there are also many large coffee, sugar cane, and tea plantations. Massive forests provide timber such as teak which is a valuable export for Burma and Thailand. Bamboo is used to build houses and for making baskets.

The mountains in the north of the region are rich in minerals. Some of the world's finest precious stones are mined in Burma.

Malaysia is one of the world's largest producers of natural rubber.

Indonesia and the Philippines consists of thousands of islands. Both these countries depend on agriculture and on mining for their wealth. Singapore is an important financial and industrial center.

Tourism is a thriving industry in parts of Southeast Asia. Some visitors flock to the beaches of Thailand or Indonesia. Others shop for tax-free bargains in Singapore.

Left High-rise buildings tower over Singapore's main harbor. Although only a small island, Singapore is one of Asia's most highly developed countries, with advanced high technology industries, international banks, and a high standard of living. Its port is one of the world's busiest.

Above A village turns out to transplant rice in northern Thailand. Rice cultivation is a main source of income in Southeast Asia. Rice fields, called paddies, are flooded at the start of the growing season. The young rice plants are then transplanted and thinned out.

Rubber on tap

Rubber comes from latex, produced by rubber trees. About 85 percent of the world's natural rubber is grown in plantations in Southeast Asia. A groove is cut in the bark of a tree, about 3.3 ft (1 m) above the ground. A spout and a metal cup are positioned to collect the latex.

Right A floating market in central Thailand sells a dazzling array of fruit, vegetables, and flowers. Irrigation canals and small rivers crisscross the low plain around the mouth of the Chao Phraya River. These waterways act as thoroughfares to transport produce and other goods to market.

BRUNEI
Capital: Bandar Seri Begawan
Population: 372,000

BURMA (MYANMAR)
Capital: Rangoon
Population: 41,279,000

CAMBODIA
Capital: Phnom Penh
Population: 8,200,000

INDONESIA
Capital: Jakarta
Population: 184,300,000

LAOS
Capital: Vientiane
Population: 4,024,000

MALAYSIA
Capital: Kuala Lumpur
Population: 17,250,000

PHILIPPINES
Capital: Manila
Population: 66,647,000

SINGAPORE
Capital: Singapore
Population: 2,703,000

THAILAND
Capital: Bangkok
Population: 55,890,000

VIETNAM
Capital: Hanoi
Population: 68,488,000

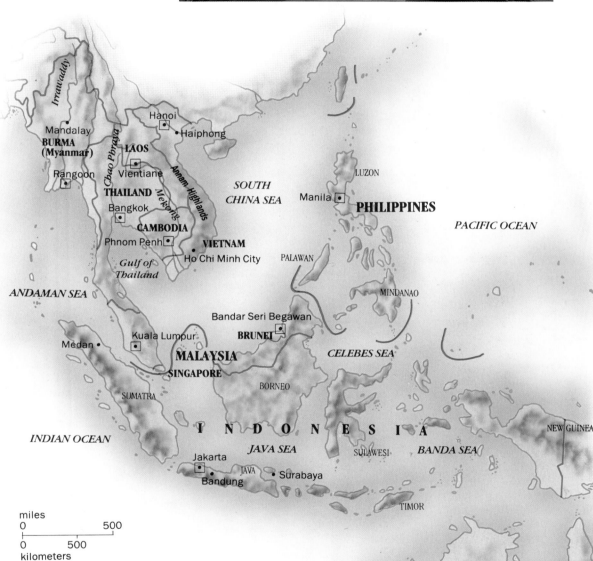

miles
0   500
0   500
kilometers

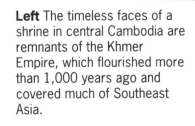

Left The timeless faces of a shrine in central Cambodia are remnants of the Khmer Empire, which flourished more than 1,000 years ago and covered much of Southeast Asia.

Right Cambodia's strong Buddhist traditions are carried on by a new generation. These young men have given up all their worldly goods to become Buddhist monks.

THE MIDDLE EAST

The Middle East occupies an area in south-western Asia. Much of the northern part of the region is covered with barren mountains and plateaus, while the south is a vast desert.

About three quarters of the people who live in the Middle East are Arabs. They share a language and culture. The rest include Turks, Armenians, Copts, Greeks, Jews, and Kurds. The Middle East is the birthplace of three major religions (Judaism, Christianity, and Islam). This has led to racial, religious, and political tension, making the area one of the most troubled in the world.

Half the people in the Middle East work small farms. The most fertile lands lie along the banks of the Jordan River, and near the Tigris and Euphrates rivers which rise in Turkey and flow through Syria and Iraq. This area, known as the Fertile Crescent, was where the Sumerian civilization developed 6,000 years ago. Here, and in irrigated areas farmers grow many crops. In barren areas, many people are nomadic herders.

Three fifths of the world's known oil reserves lie under the barren desert landscape of the Middle East. Several oil-producing states use profits from oil production to improve their industries and the living conditions of their people. But Israel, which has almost no oil, has the most advanced industries. Turkey, with little oil, is the region's most important farming country.

Below The border between Yemen and Saudi Arabia runs through the Rub' al Khali desert, which covers the lower Arabian Peninsula.

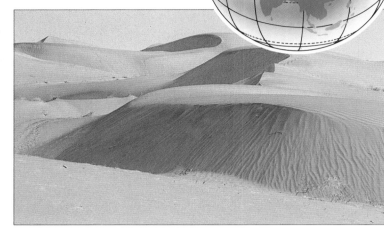

Above Thousands of Muslim pilgrims circle the Ka'aba, a sacred stone that is Islam's holiest shrine. It is in the Saudi Arabian city of Mecca.

Below Pools of water collect in extensive calcium deposits that occur in Pammokale, Turkey.

Black gold

Oil supplies over half the world's energy. Fuels made from oil provide power for ships, planes, cars, trains, and trucks. Oil is also used to generate heat and electricity. Many products, including plastics, cosmetics, medicines, and fabrics, are made from oil. Oil is so valuable that it is often referred to as "black gold." But scientists are concerned that the world's oil supplies are being used up and that by 2020 the oil wells will have run dry.

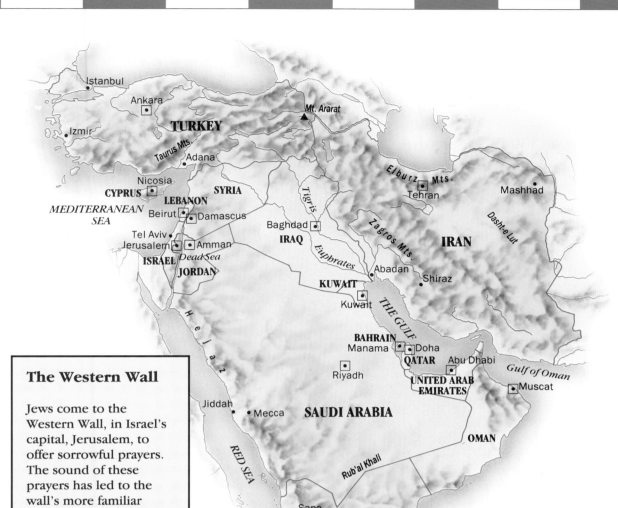

The Western Wall

Jews come to the Western Wall, in Israel's capital, Jerusalem, to offer sorrowful prayers. The sound of these prayers has led to the wall's more familiar name, the Wailing Wall. It is believed to be the remains of the western wall of Herod's temple, destroyed by the Romans in AD 70.

miles
0 — 500
0 — 500
kilometers

Left Pearl divers from Bahrain still work the waters of the Persian Gulf, but this traditional industry is now overshadowed by oil production.

Cave-dwellers

In Cappadocia in central Turkey there are villages whose inhabitants live in houses that have been carved into the soft, cone-shaped rocks. Several cave cities, perhaps first built around 4,000 years ago, have been discovered.

Left Iranians rest on their way to market in the southern town of Mirab. The woman's face is covered in keeping with Muslim tradition. Nearly all Iranians are strict believers in Islam.

BAHRAIN
Capital: Manama
Population: 512,000

CYPRUS
Capital: Nicosia
Population: 708,000

IRAN
Capital: Tehran
Population: 55,647,000

IRAQ
Capital: Baghdad
Population: 18,782,000

ISRAEL
Capital: Jerusalem
Population: 4,470,000

JORDAN
Capital: Amman
Population: 3,940,000

KUWAIT
Capital: Kuwait City
Population: 1,200,000

LEBANON
Capital: Beirut
Population: 2,700,000

OMAN
Capital: Muscat
Population: 1,305,000

QATAR
Capital: Doha
Population: 498,000

SAUDI ARABIA
Capital: Riyadh
Population: 14,000,000

SYRIA
Capital: Damascus
Population: 12,471,000

TURKEY
Capital: Ankara
Population: 56,549,000

UNITED ARAB EMIRATES
Capital: Abu Dhabi
Population: 1,600,000

YEMEN
Capital: Sana
Population: 11,500,000

SECTION 4: AFRICA

No other continent has changed as much as Africa in the course of this century. Less than 100 years ago most African countries were colonies of European powers. Today they are independent but face famine, drought, and political unrest.

INTRODUCTION

Africa is the world's second largest continent. Its population ranks third, behind Asia and Europe. There are more than 800 ethnic groups in Africa, each with its own language, beliefs, and way of life. Many African countries have rival groups living within their borders. Most of the time, these groups live peacefully, but conflicts between tribes sometimes lead to terrible civil wars.

Despite the growth of large, modern cities, most Africans still live in rural areas, where they raise livestock and grow food crops. "Cash" crops such as coffee, cocoa, and cotton are sold worldwide.

The world's largest desert, the Sahara, covers nearly one third of Africa. Many other parts of the continent receive little rainfall, and in recent years there have been severe droughts. Thousands of Africans have starved despite the aid supplied by other nations.

Many African countries have rich mineral deposits that are mined and exported. The income from these minerals has helped some countries, such as South Africa, to develop their industries. But much of the continent is still not industrialized, and many countries rely on gifts or loans of money from other governments to develop industry and agriculture.

Above About two thirds of Mali's population is Muslim. This magnificent mosque is one of the landmarks of Mopti in central Mali. The simplest building ingredients, mud and timber, have been used to create an intricate design.

Left A Berber market adds a dash of color to the city of Oued Luou in Sudan. The Berbers are native to most North African countries, and live in areas around the Sahara desert. Many of them are nomadic herders of camels, goats, sheep, and cows. Trading is an important part of Berber society.

Above The Sahara desert has a wide variety of landscapes. Here, the rippling sand dunes of the northern Sahara catch the evening sun in Morocco. With one of the harshest environments in the world, the highest temperature ever (136°F/58°C) was recorded here in 1922.

Right A bridge spans the river Nile in Cairo, the capital of Egypt. Minarets of a mosque contrast with modern tower blocks. Cairo has a population of more than 10 million, more than any other city in Africa. Nearly all of Egypt's population lives along the banks of the Nile.

THE COUNTRIES OF AFRICA

50
Algeria, Egypt, Libya, Morocco, Tunisia

52
Benin, Burkina, Cameroon, Gambia, Ghana, Guinea, Guinea-Bissau, Ivory Coast, Liberia, Mali, Mauritania, Niger, Nigeria, Senegal, Sierra Leone, Togo, Western Sahara

54
Angola, Burundi, Central African Republic, Chad, Comoros, Congo, Djibouti, Ethiopia, Equatorial Guinea, Gabon, Kenya, Madagascar, Malawi, Mauritius, Mozambique, Rwanda, São Tomé and Princípe, Seychelles, Somalia, Sudan, Tanzania, Uganda, Zaire, Zambia

56
Botswana, Lesotho, Namibia, South Africa, Swaziland, Zimbabwe

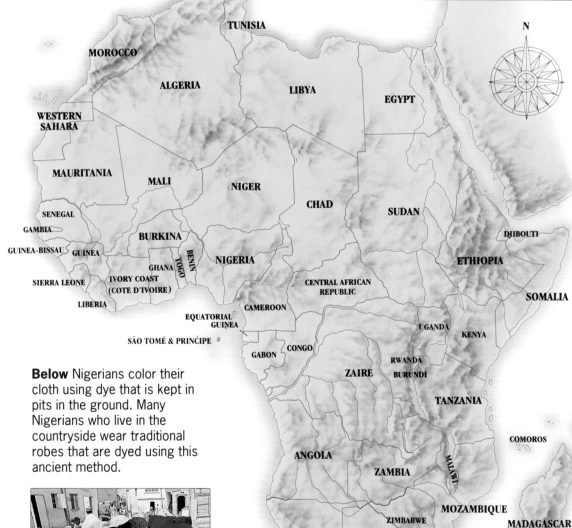

Below Nigerians color their cloth using dye that is kept in pits in the ground. Many Nigerians who live in the countryside wear traditional robes that are dyed using this ancient method.

miles
0   1000
0   1000
kilometers

Below Grapes soak up the warm sunshine in Boschendal, in the Cape Province of South Africa. Dutch and French settlers in the 17th century planted the first vines in the Cape Province, where winters are damp but never very cold. This "Mediterranean" climate is like that of Europe's chief wine-producing regions.

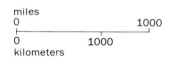

NORTH AFRICA

Egypt, Libya, Tunisia, Algeria, and Morocco all lie in the northern part of Africa. Most Moroccans, Algerians, Tunisians, and Libyans live along the fertile coastal plains where the main cities are also situated. The narrow valley of the Nile River has been home for most Egyptians for 5,000 years. It is now one of the most heavily populated regions on Earth. Egypt's capital, Cairo, is the largest and most populous city in Africa.

In the northwest lie the stony peaks of the Atlas Mountains, and the rest of the landscape is mainly desert. The Sahara Desert stretches right across the north of the continent, covering an area of 3,474,000 square miles (9,000,000 sq km). Deposits of oil, natural gas, and minerals have been discovered beneath the Sahara. Oil extraction and mining have brought wealth to the countries of North Africa, while providing a basis for the development of industry.

Despite the increased industrial development, most people in North Africa still earn a living by raising livestock and farming. The hot, dry climate means that much of the farmland has to be irrigated in order to make it fertile enough for crops to grow. Cereals, citrus fruits, olives, rice, sugar cane, dates, and cotton are all important crops for these countries.

A desert partnership

For thousands of years camels have been used to carry or pull loads and to provide a source of food. The fur is used for clothes, tents, and shelters, while the tough skin is made into shoes, saddles, and water bags. Camels are well adapted for life in the desert, and their sure footing in loose sand makes them the best form of transportation. A camel stores fat in his hump, a source of nourishment when fresh food is scarce. Spirited bargaining is typical and expected when camels are bought and sold at markets, like this one in Egypt.

Above Fishermen mend their nets and clean their fishing tackle along Morocco's Atlantic coastline. Fishing is an important industry in Morocco, which has good catches of sardines and mackerel. A number of fish canneries employ people along the Moroccan coast, from Casablanca to Agadir.

Left Shoppers and traders find shelter in the shade of date palms on market day in Douz, an oasis settlement in southern Tunisia. The traditional white, loose-fitting clothing is cooling in the fierce heat of the Sahara. After many hours of high-spirited bargaining, the market draws to a close.

Above The farming community of Ureka lies in the High Atlas Mountains of Morocco. This range is the highest in northwest Africa and forms a barrier with the Sahara.

The world's longest river

The Nile has two main branches, the White Nile and the Blue Nile, which join together at Khartoum in Sudan. The source of the Nile has been traced to the Ruvironza River in Burundi. From Burundi, the Nile flows for 4,137 miles (6,671 km) to its delta on the Mediterranean Sea.

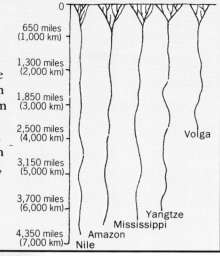

0
650 miles (1,000 km)
1,300 miles (2,000 km)
1,850 miles (3,000 km)
2,500 miles (4,000 km)
3,150 miles (5,000 km)
3,700 miles (6,000 km)
4,350 miles (7,000 km)

Volga
Yangtze
Mississippi
Amazon
Nile

ALGERIA
Capital: Algiers
Population: 25,714,000

EGYPT
Capital: Cairo
Population: 54,139,000

LIBYA
Capital: Tripoli
Population: 4,280,000

MOROCCO
Capital: Rabat
Population: 26,249,000

TUNISIA
Capital: Tunis
Population: 8,094,000

Tangier
Algiers
Tunis
Oran
Batna
Sousse
Rabat
Casablanca
MEDITERRANEAN SEA
Marrakesh
High Atlas Mts.
TUNISIA
ATLANTIC OCEAN
Agadir
MOROCCO
Tripoli
Benghazi
Port Said
Alexandria
Suez Canal
Cairo
ALGERIA
Sahara
LIBYA
Libyan Desert
EGYPT
Ahaggar Mts.
Nile
Aswan

miles
0   500
0   500
kilometers

Below A group of Bedouin tents provides shelter in the desert. Bedouins are nomadic people of the Middle East.

The sands of time

Egypt was the birthplace of one of the world's earliest civilizations. The ancient Egyptians, whose empire flourished between 3000 and 1000 BC, lived along the banks of the Nile. They developed a form of picture writing called hieroglyphics and invented paper made from papyrus reeds. They built massive stone temples and pyramids, as tombs for the Egyptian kings, the Pharaohs. Today, the ancient Egyptian ruins along the Nile River attract thousands of visitors.

Most people in Egypt make their living by farming and keeping cattle.

WEST AFRICA

West Africa has four distinct types of landscape, each running east to west. The Sahara desert extends into the region's northernmost countries, Western Sahara, Mauritania, Mali, Niger, and Chad. These countries have small populations, which make their living mainly from herding. Senegal and the Gambia lie on the Sahara's western edge, but have fertile farmland nearer the Atlantic.

Along the southern edge of the Sahara is a dry grassland known as the Sahel. This becomes the Western Plateau, an area of forests and grasslands. The southern edge of the region is coastal plains and jungles.

Nigeria extends southwards from the Sahel to the coast. It is the region's most developed country, and has the largest population in Africa. Income from large oil deposits has helped the Nigerians build petrochemical and steel industries.

Nigeria's chief port, Lagos, is a trading center for Guinea-Bissau, Guinea, Sierra Leone, Liberia, Ivory Coast, Burkina, Ghana, Togo, Benin, and Cameroon. Most people in these countries are farmers, although some industries have developed around Abidjan and Accra. Sierra Leone also has diamond and bauxite mines.

Below A Fulani herder tends his goats and cattle in Senegal. The Fulani are a nomadic people for whom livestock is the chief source of income. They are of mixed Mediterranean and African descent and are scattered across West Africa, from Senegal to Cameroon.

Above Mending traditional fishing nets is a painstaking business. This fisherman lives on the Gold Coast, a part of Ghana that lies on the Gulf of Guinea. The British named this area the Gold Coast in the 18th century after seeing the intricate goldwork produced by local craftsmen.

Left Villagers need a canoe to paddle from house to house in this village in Benin. Stilt houses offer protection from wild animals as well as flood waters. Benin has a dramatic rainy season when water levels on lakes rise and rivers can turn to torrents overnight. Even young children must learn to maneuver canoes.

Precious storehouses

Farming can be an unpredictable occupation in West Africa. Drought is a constant threat in an area so near the Sahara. Equally destructive are heavy rains, which can destroy crops in the fields and cause harvested crops to rot. Another threat to farmers is rats.

Most West African farmers store their harvests in specially designed granaries like this one in Senegal (left) used to store couscous. The buildings are on stilts because they are prone to flooding. The Dogon people in Mali store their millet high up on hillsides (right) in granaries that resemble caves.

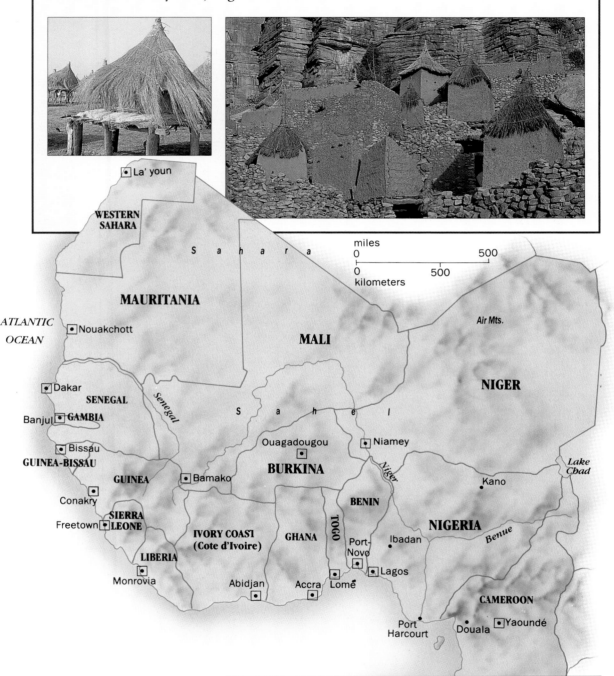

BENIN
Capital: Port Novo
Population: 4,840,000

BURKINA
Capital: Ouagadougou
Population: 8,941,000

CAMEROON
Capital: Yaoundé
Population: 11,900,000

GAMBIA
Capital: Banjul
Population: 860,000

GHANA
Capital: Accra
Population: 15,310,000

GUINEA
Capital: Conakry
Population: 7,269,000

GUINEA-BISSAU
Capital: Bissau
Population: 998,000

IVORY COAST (COTE D'IVOIRE)
Capital: Abidjan
Population: 12,070,000

LIBERIA
Capital: Monrovia
Population: 2,644,000

MALI
Capital: Bamako
Population: 8,156,000

MAURITANIA
Capital: Nouakchott
Population: 2,038,000

NIGER
Capital: Niamey
Population: 7,691,000

NIGERIA
Capital: Lagos
Population: 108,500,000

SENEGAL
Capital: Dakar
Population: 7,740,000

SIERRA LEONE
Capital: Freetown
Population: 4,168,000

TOGO
Capital: Lomé
Population: 3,566,000

WESTERN SAHARA
Capital: La'youn
Population: 175,000

Right Lagos is the largest city in Nigeria, with a population of more than 1.3 million. It is also the most important port in West Africa. Lagos-based companies trade not only Nigeria's own industrial and petrochemical products but many agricultural products from neighboring countries. Industrial plants in Lagos also harness power from Nigeria's other energy sources – coal and hydroelectricity.

CENTRAL AND EAST AFRICA

The region of Central and East Africa has a landscape of extremes. It ranges from desert to swamp, from tropical rain forest to high volcanic mountains, and from rolling grassland to deep valleys. Lake Victoria, the world's third largest lake, lies on the borders of Uganda, Kenya, and Tanzania. The snowcapped peak of Mount Kilimanjaro, Africa's highest mountain, towers over the plains of northern Tanzania. The Congo River cuts across the western part of Central Africa from its source in Zaire to the Atlantic Ocean.

The people also differ greatly. Many of the Tutsi people of Rwanda and Burundi are more than 7 feet (2.13 m) tall. By contrast, very few Pygmy people of Zaire's forests are more than 5 feet (1.5 m) tall. Some, such as the Masai of Kenya, the Efe of Zaire, and the Afar nomads of Ethiopia, follow traditional ways of life. Most survive by hunting and growing crops such as coffee, tea, corn, and other grains. Other Central and East African peoples live in modern cities such as Nairobi, Kenya's capital.

Most countries in Central and East Africa are poor, and what wealth they have comes from the export of foodstuffs such as coffee. Timber is an important export for those countries which are covered by large areas of rain forest. Kenya now has a wide variety of industries, including steel and textiles, while Zaire and Zambia are rich in minerals.

"The cradle of civilization"

The Great Rift Valley stretches from Syria to Mozambique. It is a series of valleys, formed by movements of the plates of rock which make up the Earth's crust. The Rift system separates into two branches. Fossil remains of very early humans have been found along the Great Rift Valley which is referred to as the "cradle of civilization".

Below Whole families turn out at low tide to dig for shellfish along the Mozambique coast of Quelimane. The village of Quelimane lies just north of the mouth of the Zambezi River.

Above The peak of Mount Kilimanjaro rises majestically out of the plains of Tanzania. The highest mountain in Africa, at 19,340 ft (5,895 m) Kilimanjaro is an active volcano.

Left Kenya's population is made up of many different tribes, each with its own set of customs and language. Special rituals and celebrations help maintain cultural links with the past. This Masai dance mirrors the act of a hunt.

Right The colors of some African handicrafts are dazzling. These fabrics and shoes are being sold in a market in Mozambique's capital, Maputo. To the side is a selection of intricately carved wooden figures.

COMOROS
Capital: Moroni
Population: 551,000

CONGO
Capital: Brazzaville
Population: 2,305,000

DJIBOUTI
Capital: Djibouti
Population: 530,000

EQUATORIAL GUINEA
Capital: Malabo
Population: 420,000

CHAD
Capital: N'Djamena
Population: 5,400,000

ETHIOPIA
Capital: Addis Ababa
Population: 51,375,000

C. AFRICAN REP.
Capital: Bangui
Population: 2,879,000

GABON
Capital: Libreville
Population: 1,210,000

KENYA
Capital: Nairobi
Population: 25,393,000

BURUNDI
Capital: Bujumbura
Population: 5,647,000

MADAGASCAR
Capital: Antananarivo
Population: 11,802,000

ANGOLA
Capital: Luanda
Population: 9,500,000

MALAWI
Capital: Lilongwe
Population: 9,080,000

MAURITIUS
Capital: Port Louis
Population: 1,141,900

Above In Sudan, camels are still important. Here traders assemble outside Omdurman, Sudan's largest city.

MOZAMBIQUE
Capital: Maputo
Population: 14,718,000

RWANDA
Capital: Kigali
Population: 7,603,000

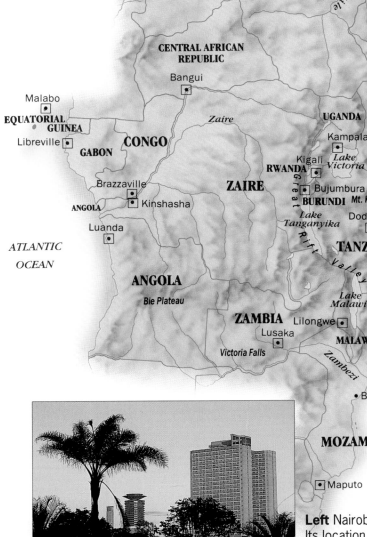

SÃO TOMÉ AND PRINCÍPE
Capital: São Tomé
Population: 125,000

SEYCHELLES
Capital: Victoria
Population: 71,000

SOMALIA
Capital: Mogadishu
Population: 8,415,000

SUDAN
Capital: Khartoum
Population: 25,164,000

TANZANIA
Capital: Dodoma
Population: 26,070,000

UGANDA
Capital: Kampala
Population: 17,593,000

ZAIRE
Capital: Kinshasha
Population: 35,330,000

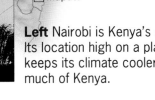

Left Nairobi is Kenya's capital. Its location high on a plateau keeps its climate cooler than much of Kenya.

ZAMBIA
Capital: Lusaka
Population: 8,119,000

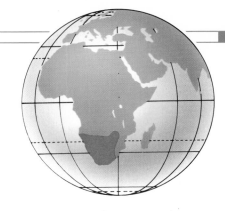

SOUTHERN AFRICA

Much of Southern Africa is covered by a vast area of rolling grassland known as the Southern Plateau. The Kalahari and Namib deserts cover most of the northern interior and western coast of the region. A lowland strip along the continent's southeast coast is extremely fertile.

South Africa is the southernmost country in Africa. Its position as the world's largest gold producer means that it is also the continent's richest and most powerful country. South Africa produces two fifths of Africa's manufactured goods, nearly half of its minerals and one fifth of its agricultural products. Industry is concentrated around Johannesburg and Pretoria, as well as Cape Town, Port Elizabeth, and Durban.

For many years, life in South Africa was based on a policy known as apartheid, which gave few rights to the black people who make up two thirds of the country's population. This is now changing.

Namibia and Botswana lie on the Namib and Kalahari deserts. They rely on minerals for their incomes, although most people live on dry, dusty farms. Botswana is now one of the world's largest producers of diamonds.

Zimbabwe also has mineral resources, as well as extensive tobacco, sugar, and cotton farms. Its landlocked position means that Zimbabwean producers must rely on South Africa or Mozambique to export their goods.

The region's other two landlocked countries, Lesotho and Swaziland, have few natural resources. Lesotho relies on agriculture and the income earned by its migrant workers in South Africa. Swaziland is gradually replacing agriculture with manufacturing as its main source of income.

Left Victoria Falls, along the Zambezi River, forms part of the border between Zambia and Zimbabwe.

Right A nature warden wears protective clothing to handle a poisonous snake found near Port Elizabeth, South Africa.

Below Durban is the largest city and chief port of Natal Province, along South Africa's Indian Ocean coastline.

South Africa's gold

South Africa is the world's largest producer of gold. To reach the gold, miners dig deep shafts then dig or drill into the rock. Once the rock has been dug out, it is taken to mills where the gold is separated from the rock by machine or by the use of chemicals. The gold is smelted (heated in a furnace) to remove impurities. The pure gold that remains is cast into bars.

BOTSWANA
Capital: Gaborone
Population: 1,300,000

LESOTHO
Capital: Maseru
Population: 1,757,000

NAMIBIA
Capital: Windhoek
Population: 1,372,000

SOUTH AFRICA
Capital: Cape Town
Population: 39,550,000

SWAZILAND
Capital: Mbabane
Population: 779,000

ZIMBABWE
Capital: Harare
Population: 10,205,000

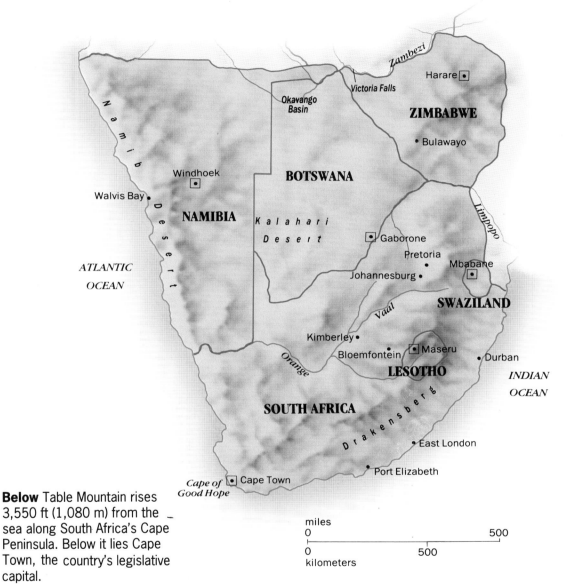

miles
0 _____ 500
0 _____ 500
kilometers

Below Table Mountain rises 3,550 ft (1,080 m) from the sea along South Africa's Cape Peninsula. Below it lies Cape Town, the country's legislative capital.

Heart of an empire

Zimbabwe takes its name from Great Zimbabwe, a 58-acre (24-hectare) complex of stone ruins near the town of Nyanda. Parts of this settlement and fortress are nearly 1,300 years old. The builders had to carve the heavy stones with great skill because no mortar was used to hold them together. From about AD 1000 to 1400 Great Zimbabwe was the center of an inland empire ruled by the Karanga people. Karanga goods, such as gold ornaments and sandstone carvings, were traded for goods from Asia.

SECTION 5: NORTH AND CENTRAL AMERICA

The abundant resources of North America have helped the United States become one of the world's most powerful countries. Canada also has a high standard of living, but life is harder in Mexico and Central America.

INTRODUCTION

North and Central America form the third largest continent. The extreme north lies within the bitter cold of the Arctic Circle. Hot, steamy rain forests and volcanic mountains form the landscape of Central America. In between there are grasslands, mountains, lakes, and deserts.

North America is divided into Canada, the United States of America, and Mexico. South of Mexico lie the countries of Central America (Belize, Honduras, Guatemala, El Salvador, Nicaragua, and Costa Rica).

North America has vast supplies of natural resources and huge expanses of fertile farmland. These factors, as well as its many highly successful industries, have helped make the United States the world's leading economic power. Canada also has a high standard of living. Central America, by contrast, has few natural resources and little fertile farmland. Many people are poor.

Most North Americans are of European descent, but there are also descendants of immigrants from many other parts of the world as well as North American Indians. Most people in Mexico and Central America are of Spanish and American Indian descent.

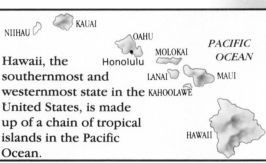

Left The United States Air Force Academy football team takes on the opposition at its stadium in Colorado Springs, high up in the Rocky Mountains. Football now rivals baseball as the most popular sport in the United States.

Hawaii, the southernmost and westernmost state in the United States, is made up of a chain of tropical islands in the Pacific Ocean.

NIIHAU KAUAI OAHU MOLOKAI PACIFIC OCEAN Honolulu LANAI MAUI KAHOOLAWE HAWAII

ALASKA (US)

Left The distinctive rock formations that rise from the floor of Monument Valley are familiar to film-lovers as the backdrops to many westerns. These rocky outcrops, which lie on the border between Arizona and Utah, were formed by thousands of years of erosion and geological upheaval. The scientific name for such an outcrop is a butte.

Above Colorful floats, dancers, and jazz bands lead the lively Mardi Gras procession in New Orleans, Louisiana's great port on the Mississippi River. The festival carries on a tradition started by Louisiana's Spanish and French settlers more than 250 years ago. It builds to a climax on the Tuesday before the Christian period of Lent.

Above Massive ice cliffs overhang a tour boat in Glacier Bay, Alaska.

Right These totem poles tell the tribal histories of Indians in the Canadian province of British Columbia.

THE COUNTRIES OF NORTH AND CENTRAL AMERICA

—60—
Canada, Greenland

—62—
United States of America

—66—
Antigua, Bahamas, Barbados, Belize, Costa Rica, Cuba, Dominica, Dominican Republic, El Salvador, Grenada, Guatemala, Haiti, Honduras, Jamaica, Mexico, Netherlands Antilles, Nicaragua, Panama, Puerto Rico, St. Kitts-Nevis, Saint Lucia, St. Vincent and Grenadines, Trinidad and Tobago

GREENLAND

miles
0 _____ 1000
0 _____ 1000
kilometers

CANADA

UNITED STATES

MEXICO

BAHAMAS

CUBA

JAMAICA

HAITI

DOMINICAN REPUBLIC

GUATEMALA BELIZE

HONDURAS

EL SALVADOR

NICARAGUA

COSTA RICA

PANAMA

Right The mirrored walls of the John Hancock Tower in Boston reflect the facade of a much older building. The tower is Boston's tallest skyscraper.

Right People from neighboring villages mingle with local inhabitants when Mexican towns such as Taxco close their streets for a market or a religious fiesta.

Right The Caribbean island of St. Lucia is one of the most beautiful in a group known as the Lesser Antilles. Great rocks, called Pitons, stand at the southern end of the island. Dense vegetation, some of it almost rain forest, covers the slopes of the Pitons all the way down to the water's edge. The Pitons are the remains of volcanic cones.

Left Wildflowers and pine forests line the shore of Lake Louise in the Canadian province of Alberta. The lake is part of Banff National Park, one of the most popular recreation areas in the Canadian Rockies. The town of Banff is a sophisticated resort.

CANADA AND GREENLAND

Much of northern Canada is uninhabited or only thinly populated because of the rugged, mountainous landscape and severe climate. About 80 percent of Canada's population lives within 200 miles (320 km) of the border with the United States. This population is made up of a wide racial mix. It includes people of British and French descent, as well as other Europeans, immigrants from the Far East, and North American Indians, and Inuit.

Canada is rich in natural resources, which provide food and export income. This wealth derives from logging and wood-processing industries, mining, agriculture, and fishing.

The western part of Canada is a region of outstanding natural beauty, dominated by the towering Rocky Mountains and deep forests in the foothills. The logging and wood-processing industries are concentrated there.

The fertile center of Canada is known as the "prairies." Vast fields of wheat stretch as far as the eye can see, and cattle and pigs are raised in the millions. Farther east, the areas bordering the Great Lakes are the most densely populated and industrialized parts of the country. Wood products, newsprint, chemicals, and steel are produced. Quebec, Canada's largest province in area, preserves

Quebec's sweet trickle

Maple syrup is produced by boiling the sap from sugar maple trees. This technique has remained largely unchanged for centuries. The sap is collected in late winter and early spring. Pure maple syrup is expensive because a great deal of sap is needed to produce a small amount of syrup. (Most pancake syrups use only a small amount of maple syrup.) Quebec is the leading producer of maple syrup.

Above Winter sports are popular throughout Canada. Families turn out to skate along the river that runs beside the Canadian Houses of Parliament in Ottawa, the national capital. The city is near the Quebec-Ontario border.

its French culture and language. The Atlantic Provinces support important fishing and mining industries.

Greenland, the world's largest island, lies off the northeast coast of Canada. Greenland is officially part of Denmark. Most of the island is a plateau, which is permanently covered with ice. Only 16 percent of Greenland's total land area is ice-free. Most of the population lives near the island's southwestern coast, and earns a living by fishing and fish processing.

People of the Arctic

The Inuit (or Eskimo) live in Greenland and in the northern parts of North America. The word "Eskimo," means "eaters of raw meat." The earliest Inuit moved around in family groups, hunting and fishing. In summer, they lived in tents and in winter, in igloos built from blocks of snow. Today, most Inuit live in modern wooden houses. Some still survive by hunting seals and caribou.

CANADA
Capital: Ottawa
Population: 26,620,000

GREENLAND
Capital: Godthaab
Population: 55,000

Left A bridal party, dressed in traditional hand-knit sweaters and leggings, arrives at the church for a wedding in Greenland. The bride carries a bouquet of plastic flowers because real flowers cannot survive the harsh Greenland climate in winter.

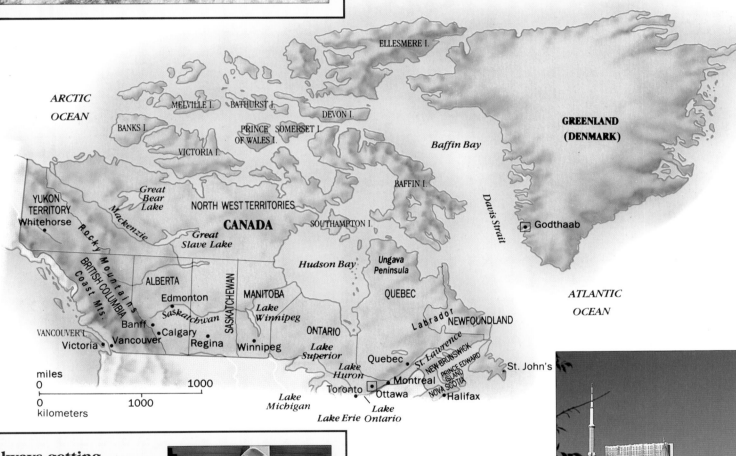

ARCTIC OCEAN

ELLESMERE I.

MELVILLE I. BATHURST I. DEVON I.

BANKS I. PRINCE SOMERSET I. OF WALES I.

VICTORIA I.

Baffin Bay

GREENLAND (DENMARK)

BAFFIN I.

YUKON TERRITORY
Whitehorse

Great Bear Lake

Mackenzie

NORTH WEST TERRITORIES

SOUTHAMPTON I.

Davis Strait

Godthaab

CANADA

Great Slave Lake

Rocky Mountains

BRITISH COLUMBIA

Coast Mts.

ALBERTA

Edmonton

Saskatchewan

Hudson Bay

Ungava Peninsula

SASKATCHEWAN

MANITOBA

QUEBEC

ATLANTIC OCEAN

Banff

Calgary

Lake Winnipeg

Labrador

NEWFOUNDLAND

VANCOUVER I.
Victoria Vancouver

Regina

Winnipeg

ONTARIO

Lake Superior

Quebec

St. Lawrence

NEW BRUNSWICK

St. John's

miles
0   1000
0   1000
kilometers

Lake Huron

Lake Michigan

Toronto Ottawa
Montreal

PRINCE EDWARD ISLAND

NOVA SCOTIA

Halifax

Lake Erie Ontario

Always getting their men

The Royal Canadian Mounted Police (RCMP) are the federal police force of Canada. The force was established in 1873 to maintain law and order in Canada's western plains. Members became known as "Mounties" because they traveled on horseback.

Right Canada's largest city, Toronto, has a lively mixture of old and new buildings. The red-brick building and gas lamp in the foreground belong to the 19th century. Behind are modern skyscrapers, and the CN Tower, at 1,821 ft (555 m), the world's tallest self-supporting structure.

EASTERN UNITED STATES

In the northeastern corner of the United States is the region of New England, famous for its picturesque villages, fishing harbors, and beautiful autumn scenery. Much of New England is too hilly or too rocky for growing crops, but dairy cattle and poultry are raised. Fishing is also important.

The Middle Atlantic States, the most densely populated area of the country, lie south of New England along the coast. Deepwater harbors have helped make the region a major center of international trade. The busiest port is New York City, the largest city in the country. It is also a national and world leader in finance, industry, advertising, and the arts.

The Eastern United States also includes some of the states of the fertile inland region known as the Midwest. Here, industrial cities such as Chicago and Detroit benefit from the region's efficient transportation network provided by the Mississippi River system, the Great Lakes, and numerous railroads.

The Southern States are characterized by rolling hills, forested mountains, and coastal plains. The beaches along the Atlantic Ocean and the Gulf of Mexico attract many tourists. Industry has boomed in recent years, and the region no longer relies quite so heavily on the production of tobacco and cotton.

The seat of government

Washington, D.C., is the capital of the United States. It takes up all of the District of Columbia (D.C.), an area specially set aside in 1790 as the nation's capital. The "founding fathers" wanted to ensure that no state could claim to have the national capital within its borders. The city is named after President George Washington, who chose its site in 1791. Washington, D.C., opened as the capital in 1800. It has many impressive monuments and buildings, including the White House, the President's residence, and the Capitol (right).

Above Paddle-driven steamboats recall the romantic days of the "Old South." These boats now only survive as tourist attractions, but in the 19th century they were the fastest way of traveling along the Mississippi and Missouri rivers.

Left The twin towers of the World Trade Center are the tallest buildings in New York City. Most of New York's skyscrapers are on the island of Manhattan, where property became scarce and expensive at the end of the last century. Architects responded by building up rather than out.

UNITED STATES OF AMERICA
Capital: Washington, D.C.
Population: 248,709,873

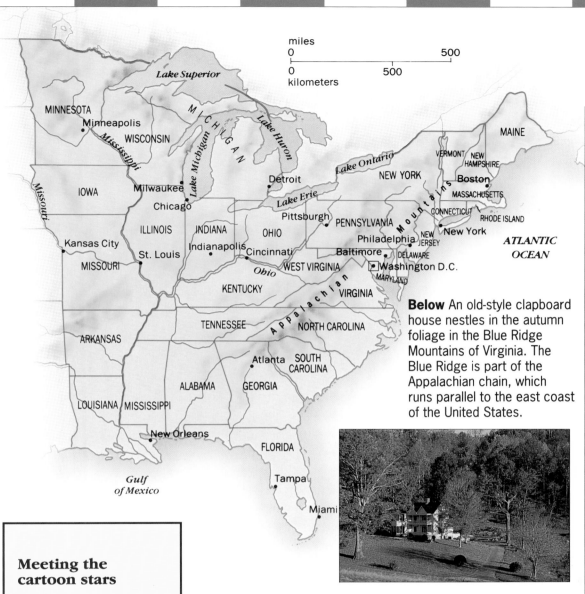

miles
0   500

0   500
kilometers

MINNESOTA
Minneapolis
WISCONSIN
Mississippi
Lake Superior
MICHIGAN
Lake Huron
Lake Michigan
Lake Ontario
Lake Erie
Detroit
Milwaukee
Chicago
IOWA
Missouri
ILLINOIS
INDIANA
OHIO
Pittsburgh
PENNSYLVANIA
Kansas City
St. Louis
Indianapolis
Cincinnati
WEST VIRGINIA
Ohio
MISSOURI
KENTUCKY
VIRGINIA
Appalachian
Mountains
MAINE
VERMONT
NEW HAMPSHIRE
NEW YORK
Boston
MASSACHUSETTS
CONNECTICUT
RHODE ISLAND
New York
NEW JERSEY
Philadelphia
Baltimore
DELAWARE
Washington D.C.
MARYLAND
ATLANTIC OCEAN
ARKANSAS
TENNESSEE
NORTH CAROLINA
ALABAMA
GEORGIA
Atlanta
SOUTH CAROLINA
LOUISIANA
MISSISSIPPI
New Orleans
FLORIDA
Tampa
Miami
Gulf of Mexico

Below An old-style clapboard house nestles in the autumn foliage in the Blue Ridge Mountains of Virginia. The Blue Ridge is part of the Appalachian chain, which runs parallel to the east coast of the United States.

Reaching for the sky

The United States set up NASA (the National Aeronautics and Space Administration) in 1958. On July 21, 1969, the Americans Neil Armstrong and "Buzz" Aldrin became the first humans to walk on the moon. Then came the development of a space station, Skylab (now fallen from orbit), and the space shuttle. Long-distance unmanned space probes travel into space to gather information in our solar system and beyond. The Kennedy Space Center at Cape Canaveral in Florida is NASA's main launch site.

Meeting the cartoon stars

Donald Duck and other Disney favorites lead a parade in Walt Disney World's Magic Kingdom in Orlando, Florida. Millions of people visit Disney World and the neighboring EPCOT Center each year, making them among the world's most popular tourist attractions. The idea for the theme park came from the popular film-maker Walt Disney.

Above Lovers of Dixieland jazz flock to Preservation Hall in New Orleans, Louisiana. The city is famous for its good-natured jazz bands that lead parades during the Mardi Gras festival and play at funerals.

Right Families eye a row of pumpkins at a farm in New York state. Americans enjoy pumpkins in sweet pies and pumpkins carved into Halloween jack-o'-lanterns.

WESTERN UNITED STATES

The Rocky Mountains dominate the western part of the United States. The region's most important state, California, lies west of the Rocky Mountains, along the Pacific coast. California earns more money from tourism than any other state, thanks to its mixture of mountains, redwood forests, deserts, and beautiful coastline. It also leads the country in farming income, and is among the leading industrial and mining states.

Washington and Oregon depend on their huge evergreen forests for income. Nevada, Utah, and Arizona consist largely of desert, although sites such as the Grand Canyon attract many tourists.

East of the Rockies lie the fertile grasslands of the Great Plains. Farther south are the wide open spaces of Texas and New Mexico. Cattle ranching has been important since cowboy times. Texas has huge reserves of oil and natural gas.

Alaska and Hawaii have only been states for about 30 years. Alaska is the largest state in area and one of the world's most important oil-producing regions. Hawaii is a popular tourist destination, and its farmers grow many tropical fruits such as pineapples.

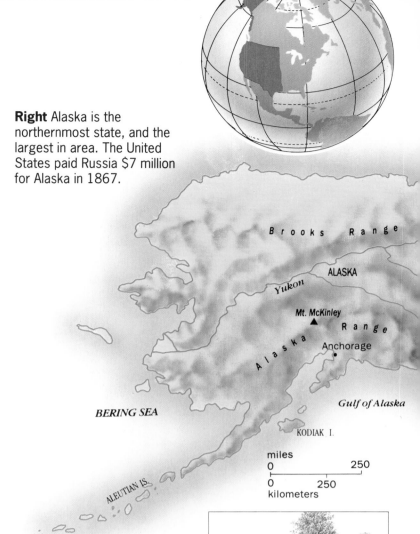

Right Alaska is the northernmost state, and the largest in area. The United States paid Russia $7 million for Alaska in 1867.

Right Giant evergreen trees called sequoias thrive in the mountains of central California. Some sequoias, such as this one in Sequoia National Park, grow as high as 300 ft (91 m).

Below Wyoming ranchers lead their cattle into a feed lot. The poor soil on Wyoming's high plains means that farms must be very big — on average more than ten times larger than those of California and Iowa.

Secrets of the stars

The studios of the major motion picture and television companies are major tourist attractions in Los Angeles. Visitors can get a behind-the-scenes look at film-making techniques. "Insiders" explain how they can set up special effects without hurting anybody. These spectators are watching a bar-room brawl staged at Universal Studios.

Above Bright neon signs attract gamblers to the famous casinos of Las Vegas, Nevada. Gambling and tourism are the chief sources of income in Nevada.

Above The faces of Presidents Washington, Jefferson, Lincoln, and Theodore Roosevelt have been carved from the granite side of Mount Rushmore in South Dakota.

Left The Grand Canyon, along the Colorado River in Arizona, is one of the world's natural wonders. The 200-mile (320-km) long canyon is more than 1 mile (1.6 km) deep

A fight to the finish

In March 1836, a Catholic mission station called the Alamo in San Antonio, Texas, became the scene of an historic battle. Texans wanted their independence from Mexico. A Mexican army marched to San Antonio to stamp out the rebellion. A tiny band of Texans, including folk heroes such as Davy Crockett and Jim Bowie, retreated to the Alamo, but were all killed after a brave fight. Texas finally joined the Union of American states in 1845. "Remember the Alamo" became a battle cry.

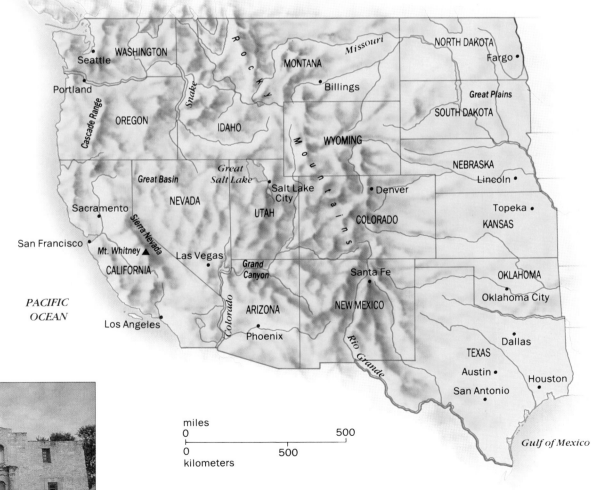

MEXICO, CENTRAL AMERICA, AND THE CARIBBEAN

Mexico is a land of contrasts. High plateaus and snowcapped mountains cover more than two-thirds of the country, but there are also tropical forests in the southeast, arid deserts in the northwest and fertile farmland in the south. Most Mexicans live in the central region, particularly in the capital, Mexico City, which is the world's second largest city.

Although only one eighth of Mexico's land is suitable for crops, agriculture employs more than 25 percent of the working population. Mexico is rich in natural resources. It is one of the world's leading silver producers and has large deposits of oil, natural gas, copper, gold, lead, and sulphur.

The Caribbean Sea is part of the Atlantic Ocean. Its thousands of islands draw millions of tourists each year. They are attracted by the sandy beaches, lush scenery, and tropical climate. The islanders earn their living mainly through tourism, farming, and fishing. Crops such as sugar cane, bananas, and citrus fruits are grown for export.

Most people in Central America are poor. Much of the land is mountainous, but coffee and bananas are grown on plantations in the lowland areas along the coasts. Timber is an important industry in Honduras, Costa Rica, and Panama. The most valuable timber export is mahogany, which is used in a wide range of high quality furniture.

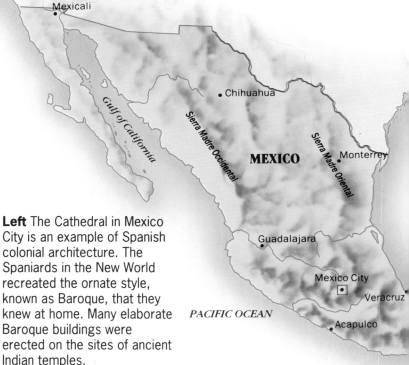

Left The Cathedral in Mexico City is an example of Spanish colonial architecture. The Spaniards in the New World recreated the ornate style, known as Baroque, that they knew at home. Many elaborate Baroque buildings were erected on the sites of ancient Indian temples.

Linking the oceans

The Panama Canal, which opened in 1914, connects the Atlantic and Pacific oceans at the Isthmus of Panama. It is 50 miles (81.6 km) long. Ships can save 8,700 miles (14,000 km) by avoiding the long route around South America. The canal was built by the United States, which still operates it. Panama will gain control of the canal in the year 2000.

Right This shepherd from Todos Santos in Guatemala works the same fields that his ancestors did more than 1,500 years ago. Many Guatemalans are descendants of the Maya and other Indian people whose civilizations were thriving long before the Spanish arrived. Many Indian customs have been maintained.

ANTIGUA AND BARBUDA
Capital: St. John's
Population: 80,000

BAHAMAS
Capital: Nassau
Population: 251,000

BARBADOS
Capital: Bridgetown
Population: 260,000

BELIZE
Capital: Belmopan
Population: 180,400

Right Chichen Itza is a Mayan ruin in eastern Mexico. Built around AD 600, it remained a seat of government and religion for over 800 years.

Below Playa Grande is one of the many unspoiled beaches along the coast of the Dominican Republic.

Above The unpolluted waters of the Caribbean are ideal for scuba divers and snorkelers. Schools of colorful tropical fish thrive in the coral reefs, which also contain sunken pirate treasure.

COSTA RICA
Capital: San José
Population: 3,032,000

CUBA
Capital: Havana
Population: 10,582,000

DOMINICA
Capital: Roseau
Population: 85,000

DOMINICAN REPUBLIC
Capital: Santo Domingo
Population: 7,253,000

EL SALVADOR
Capital: San Salvador
Population: 5,221,000

GRENADA
Capital: St. George's
Population: 104,000

GUATEMALA
Capital: Guatemala City
Population: 9,340,000

HAITI
Capital: Port-au-Prince
Population: 5,862,000

HONDURAS
Capital: Tegucigalpa
Population: 5,261,000

JAMAICA
Capital: Kingston
Population: 2,513,000

MEXICO
Capital: Mexico City
Population: 88,335,000

NICARAGUA
Capital: Managua
Population: 3,606,000

PANAMA
Capital: Panama City
Population: 2,423,000

ST.KITTS AND NEVIS
Capital: Basseterre
Population: 49,000

SAINT LUCIA
Capital: Castries
Population: 153,000

SAINT VINCENT AND GRENADINES
Capital: Kingstown
Population: 106,000

TRINIDAD AND TOBAGO
Capital: Port of Spain
Population: 1,270,000

Gulf of Mexico

Nassau
BAHAMAS

Havana

Campeche Yucatan
Peninsula

CUBA

TURKS & CAICOS IS. (UK)

ATLANTIC OCEAN

Greater Antilles

HAITI DOMINICAN
REPUBLIC
Port-au-Prince
Santo
Domingo

JAMAICA
Kingston

PUERTO
RICO
(US)

ANGUILLA (UK)

VIRGIN IS. ANTIGUA &
(US) (UK) BARBUDA
ST. KITTS & NEVIS MONTSERRAT (UK)

Belmopan
BELIZE

GUATEMALA
Guatemala
City

HONDURAS
Tegucigalpa

San Salvador
EL SALVADOR

NICARAGUA

Managua Lake
Nicaragua

San Jose
COSTA RICA

Panama
Canal
Panama
City
PANAMA

GUADELOUPE (Fr.)

DOMINICA

MARTINIQUE (Fr.)
ST. LUCIA

CARIBBEAN SEA

NETHERLAND
ANTILLES

BARBADOS

Lesser Antilles

ST. VINCENT &
GRENADA GRENADINES

TRINIDAD &
TOBAGO

miles
0   500

0   500
kilometers

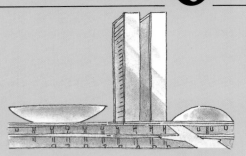

SECTION 6: SOUTH AMERICA

South America's majestic landscape includes jungles, deserts, rivers, and frozen mountains. Features such as these offer South Americans a route to new wealth, provided that they can preserve their natural inheritance.

INTRODUCTION

South America is the world's fourth largest continent. Its climate and landscape vary enormously. In the northwest is the vast basin of the Amazon River, which occupies 40 percent of South America's total land area. It is covered by dense tropical rain forest. In the south lie the pampas of Argentina, huge open plains of grass and scrubland. The snowcapped peaks and high, grassy plateaus of the Andes stretch down the west coast, from tropical Venezuela in the north to the windswept islands of Tierra del Fuego in the south. The arid Atacama Desert, one of the driest places in the world, stretches down part of the Pacific coast.

South America has rich farmland, dense forests, and huge deposits of oil and minerals such as copper, gold, lead, tin, and zinc. Coffee is a leading export crop. Despite these natural riches, many South American people are very poor. In the past, most South American countries borrowed large sums of money from other nations. The cost of repaying these loans means that there is little money for development. Millions of people have moved from the countryside into the cities in the hope of finding work. Many of the cities are overcrowded, and poverty is very widespread.

Spain and Portugal ruled most South American countries for many years. Today, although the countries are now independent most South Americans still speak Spanish or Portuguese. Some of them are descended from European settlers or from African slaves, while others are native Indians or of mixed ancestry.

Above Merchants display a wide variety of vegetables at a market in Sucre, Bolivia. The handwoven baskets hanging behind the traders are a local speciality.

Right The arid Atacama Desert covers much of the coastal region of northern Chile. The snowcapped peaks of the Andes rise up from the desert's eastern border.

Below The unmistakable peak of Sugarloaf Mountain rises 1,280 ft (390 m) at the mouth of Guanabara Bay, by the busy Brazilian port of Rio de Janeiro.

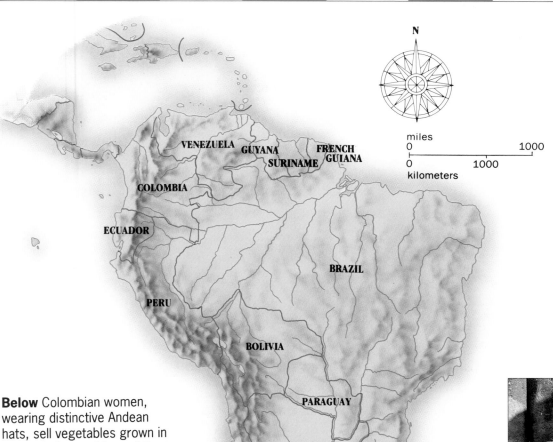

N

miles
0 · · · · · 1000

0 · · · · · 1000
kilometers

VENEZUELA · GUYANA · FRENCH GUIANA
SURINAME

COLOMBIA

ECUADOR

PERU

BRAZIL

BOLIVIA

PARAGUAY

CHILE

URUGUAY

ARGENTINA

THE COUNTRIES OF SOUTH AMERICA

——— 70 ———
Brazil, Guyana, French Guiana,
Suriname, Venezuela

——— 72 ———
Bolivia, Ecuador, Colombia, Peru

——— 74 ———
Argentina, Chile, Paraguay,
Uruguay

Below Sure-footed alpacas
have been used as pack
animals in the Andes for
thousands of years. They are
distant relatives of camels.

Below Colombian women,
wearing distinctive Andean
hats, sell vegetables grown in
mountain farms. Many of the
world's important crops,
including tomatoes, potatoes,
and tobacco, originally came
from this part of South
America.

Right Mounted ranchers,
called gauchos, round up
cattle in the Mendoza Province
of western Argentina. They
traditionally use a bola, which
is a strong rope with weights
attached to each end.
Gauchos use the bola in the
same way that North American
cowboys use a lasso. A good
throw wraps the bola around
the animal's legs, causing it to
trip without being hurt.

Above The Iguassu Falls are
one of South America's natural
wonders. They lie on the
Iguassu River, where Brazil,
Argentina, and Paraguay meet.
The sandstone has been eaten
away by the river to form a
huge basin for the waterfall.
The area around the falls is a
moist, subtropical plateau
where farmers are able to
grow sugarcane and oranges.

BRAZIL, VENEZUELA, GUYANA, SURINAME, AND FRENCH GUIANA

Brazil is the largest country in South America and the fifth largest in the world. The Amazon River flows across the north of Brazil, and much of the area is covered by the world's largest rain forest. The dry northeast of the country is mainly scrubland, but is densely populated. In the central and southern areas lie plateaus, mountain ranges, and fertile valleys, where most of Brazil's food is grown and cattle are raised. More than half of the Brazilian population lives in this region. São Paulo and Rio de Janeiro are the largest cities and manufacturing centers.

Industry has grown rapidly in Brazil in recent years. Factories produce goods ranging from appliances to cars that run on sugar. Mining is an important industry, and there are large deposits of chromium, iron, diamonds, and bauxite. Brazil is also the world's third largest producer of forest products. Almost a third of the world's coffee is produced in Brazil.

Venezuela, Guyana, Suriname, and French Guiana lie along South America's northern coast. Much of Venezuela is mountainous, but on the fertile land around the Orinoco River there are large cattle ranches and farms. This area is also the center of Venezuela's oil industry, which has brought wealth to the country. Venezuela has the largest oil deposits in South America, and is also developing the deposits of iron ore discovered in the east of the country.

Much of Guyana, Suriname, and French Guiana is covered by mountains and tropical rain forest. About half of Guyana's population is descended from plantation workers from India. Suriname was once ruled by the Netherlands. French Guiana is still a dependency of France.

The Angel Falls of Devil Mountain

The world's highest waterfall, in Venezuela, called Angel Falls, plunges a total of 3,212 ft (979 m) down the mountainside. The longest, unbroken drop is 2,648 ft (807 m). By comparison, the American falls of Niagara Falls, the world's best-known waterfall, is only 177 ft (54 m) high.

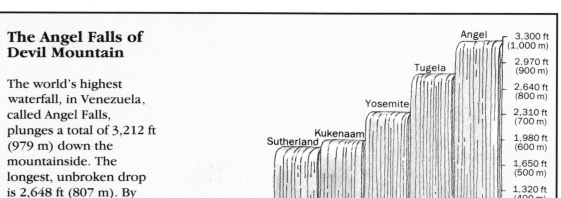

Above The colorful clothing of the shoppers and traders at Paraguaipoa's market reflects the Indian and African influences along the Caribbean coast of Venezuela. Nearly two thirds of Venezuela's population lives along the flat coastal plain, which was the first American mainland spotted by Christopher Columbus. Paraguaipoa is located on the Gulf of Venezuela near the mouth of Lake Maracaibo. The lake is one of South America's most important oil-producing centers.

Right Palm trees provide the shade along the beach at Kourou, French Guiana. Tourism is playing an important part in developing the economy of French Guiana, which is an overseas dependency of France. Its unspoiled beaches and tropical climate are distinct advantages.

BRAZIL
Capital: Brasilia
Population: 153,771,000

GUYANA
Capital: Georgetown
Population: 1,060,000

SURINAME
Capital: Paramaribo
Population: 408,000

VENEZUELA
Capital: Caracas
Population: 19,753,000

Right Dancers parade their vivid costumes during the Rio de Janeiro Carnival.

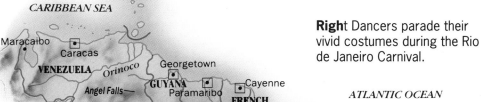

CARIBBEAN SEA

Maracaibo
Caracas
VENEZUELA
Orinoco
Georgetown
GUYANA
Paramaribo
Cayenne
Angel Falls
Guiana Highlands
SURINAME
FRENCH GUIANA
Negro
Belem
Manaus
Amazon
Madeira
Tapajos
Selvas
BRAZIL
Tocantins
Fortaleza
Recife
Salvador
Mato Grosso
Brasília
Belo Horizonte
Parana
São Paulo
Río de Janeiro
Curitiba
Porto Alegre

ATLANTIC OCEAN

miles
0   500
0   500
kilometers

Jungle highway

The building of the Trans-Amazon Highway has been a mixed blessing for Brazil. It has linked many of the remotest parts of the country's jungle interior. But the felling of trees to make the road has disturbed traditional Indian hunting grounds and destroyed the habitats of many plants and animals. Soil erosion is another serious problem.

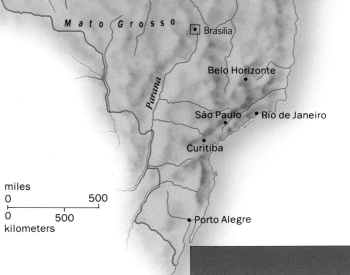

Below The National Congress is one of the many modern buildings in Brasilia, which became the capital of Brazil in 1960. Brasilia was built about 600 miles (1,000 km) inland from the major cities, São Paulo and Rio de Janeiro. The location symbolized Brazil's westward expansion.

COLOMBIA, ECUADOR, PERU, AND BOLIVIA

The Andes stretch down through the center of Colombia, Ecuador, and Peru, and dominate the western part of Bolivia. Bolivia is landlocked, but Colombia, Ecuador, and Peru all have coastal plains to the west of the Andes. Tropical rain forest covers the eastern part of all four countries.

Colombia has a coastline on both the Atlantic and Pacific oceans. Like Ecuador and Peru, it is developing its manufacturing industries. About one eighth of Colombia's population lives in Bogotá, the capital. Colombia is rich in minerals, and is the world's largest producer of emeralds.

Ecuador takes its name from its location, straddling the Equator between Colombia and Peru. Oil is the mainstay of the economy although Ecuador is also the world's largest exporter of bananas.

Indians make up about half of Peru's population. They live mainly in the Andes where they grow food and raise animals. Sugarcane and cotton are grown on the coastal plains. The rich Pacific fishing banks provide the "raw material" for Peru's largest industry–fish meal processing. Mining is also important.

Bolivia is one of the poorest countries in South America despite its rich mineral supplies. Bolivia has a large Indian population, most of whom live in the mountains.

Below Religious festivals in Ecuador are a mixture of Spanish influence and Indian traditions dating back to the days of the Incas.

Left An open-air market in Otavolo attracts people from widely scattered villages in northern Ecuador. They come to buy handicrafts and staples such as beans, corn, and grains. Music and dancing often follow the day's trading.

Right Reed boats lie at their moorings along the shore of Lake Titicaca in Bolivia. Titicaca, lying at an altitude of 12,503 ft (3,812 m), is the highest navigable lake in the world. The boats are made from totoras reeds that grow by the shore.

Beans of gold

South American coffee is famous worldwide. Coffee plants are grown on large plantations. Ripe berries are picked and washed. Each berry contains two beans. Machines remove the soft pulp from the berries, leaving only the beans and the two skins that cover them. The beans are washed and then dried in the sun. Machines remove the skins, and the beans are then sorted and roasted in large ovens. Some beans are packed in sacks and exported. Others are ground up and packed.

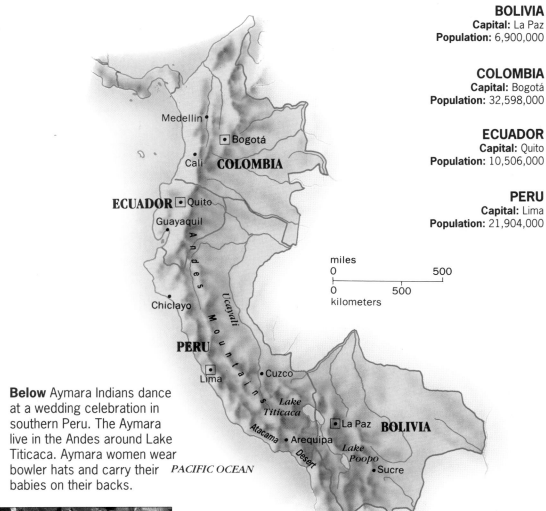

BOLIVIA
Capital: La Paz
Population: 6,900,000

COLOMBIA
Capital: Bogotá
Population: 32,598,000

ECUADOR
Capital: Quito
Population: 10,506,000

PERU
Capital: Lima
Population: 21,904,000

Below Aymara Indians dance at a wedding celebration in southern Peru. The Aymara live in the Andes around Lake Titicaca. Aymara women wear bowler hats and carry their babies on their backs.

Left A roadside vendor sells oranges in Bolivia. Most of the country's tropical fruits are grown in the river valleys lying north and east of the capital, La Paz. The extensive plains that lie east of the Andes are also developing as farming regions.

Lost city of the Andes

Machu Picchu is an ancient Incan city that stands high in the Andes. It is near the city of Cuzco in Peru. The Incas were a South American Indian people who ruled over a large and powerful empire that covered most of western South America. The empire was at the height of its power between 1450 and 1532, until it was conquered by the Spanish. The Incas were skilled engineers who built a network of roads and bridges through the Andes. They carved stone, using simple tools, and their cities contained many fine stone buildings. Because of its remote location, the city of Machu Picchu was "lost" for hundreds of years. It was rediscovered by the American explorer Hiram Bingham, in 1911.

CHILE, PARAGUAY, URUGUAY, AND ARGENTINA

Chile's landscape is dominated by the Andes, which give the country its long, narrow shape. The north of Chile is dry and barren, while the south is a wild, windswept region of rocky slopes, thick forests, and huge glaciers. Santiago, the capital, is home to over one third of Chile's population. Chile's large mineral deposits, along with its timber products, fruit, and vegetables, make up the country's main exports.

Paraguay's landlocked area is divided by the river Paraguay. Coarse grass, scrub, and salt marshes cover the western plain, called the Chaco. Ninety-five percent of the population lives in the more fertile eastern half. Paraguay is a poor country, and agriculture and forestry are the main activities. Its main exports are cotton fibers, meat, and coffee.

Gently rolling grassy plains cover most of Uruguay. Huge cattle and sheep ranches provide the country with its main exports of meat and wool. Almost half of Uruguay's population lives in Montevideo, the capital. Uruguayans traditionally enjoyed South America's highest standard of living, but problems in repaying the national debt have worsened since the 1980s.

Argentina is the second largest country in South America. The landscape changes, from the bare Patagonian plateau in the south to the forests in the north and the Andes in the west. The central area, known as the Pampas, is a fertile plain covering about one fifth of the country. Wheat, corn, and alfalfa are grown and vast herds of cattle graze on the drier areas. Most of Argentina's population lives in the Pampas region, where the country's major cities and industries are also located.

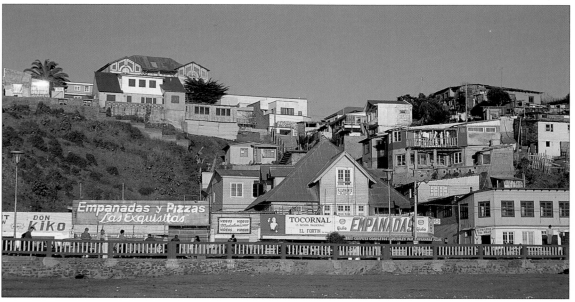

Above The lake resort of Osorno lies at the base of a volcano of the same name in southern Chile. Volcanoes are common along the whole of the Andes mountain range in South America. The sand along Osorno's lakeshore is made of crushed lava.

Left Wooden houses and shops lie on the hills above the beach at San Antonio, in central Chile. San Antonio is a popular resort and is only a short drive from Santiago, Chile's capital and largest city. Valparaiso, Chile's main port, lies just to the north.

The Atacama Desert

The Atacama Desert lies in northern Chile and the southern tip of Peru. The Atacama is one of the driest places in the world. It receives less than half an inch (1.3 cm) of rain each year, but there are parts of the desert where rain has never been recorded. Most of the desert is sand and gravel, and very few plants grow. The Atacama is rich in minerals. It is the world's only known source of natural sodium nitrate, a mineral used for making fertilizers and gunpowder. It also has large deposits of copper, iron, iodine, and other useful minerals.

ARGENTINA
Capital: Buenos Aires
Population: 32,291,000

CHILE
Capital: Santiago
Population: 13,000,000

PARAGUAY
Capital: Asunción
Population: 4,660,000

URUGUAY
Capital: Montevideo
Population: 3,002,000

Left An Indian family uses a horse and carriage to travel to Asunción, the capital of Paraguay. Landlocked Paraguay has always been one of South America's poorest countries.

Below Argentina's famous mounted ranchers, called gauchos, round up cattle in the dusty pampas. Livestock raising is one of Argentina's leading sources of income.

Left The National Park of the Glaciers preserves some of the most dramatic mountain countryside in southern Argentina. Some of the glaciers are the remnants of the last Ice Age.

Right Sheepskins are hung out to dry in Patagonia, a region in Argentina's extreme south. The *pampero*, a cold, dry wind, affects Patagonia's climate and turns the central plateau into a near-desert.

SECTION 7: THE PACIFIC

The Pacific region includes one of the continents, Australia, as well as thousands of tiny islands. Australia and New Zealand enjoy the wealth that comes from a varied economy. Most Pacific islands, though, rely on nature for their incomes.

INTRODUCTION

The Pacific is the world's largest and deepest ocean. It stretches to both polar regions and forms a wide, and largely empty, barrier between Asia and the Americas.

Australia, the largest Pacific country, is a continent itself. Its landscape and wildlife differ widely from those of other continents. Although only sparsely settled compared with other industrial countries, Australia has highly developed farming, manufacturing, and mining industries, making it the trading and commercial center for the whole of the Pacific region.

New Zealand is the largest of the island nations of the central and southern Pacific. Together they are known as Oceania. New Zealand often represents the views of the others in world affairs.

The thousands of other islands of Oceania stretch more than halfway across the Pacific. Many are remote, with populations of hardly more than a thousand and with few natural resources other than fish and coconut palms. Tourism has offered a route to more wealth.

The northern Pacific has very few islands, but the seas near China, Japan, and Siberia provide a plentiful source of fish.

Above Traditional religious beliefs remain in parts of Vanuatu, in the group of Pacific islands known as Melanesia. Ceremonies honor the spirits of the islanders' ancestors. They believe that a person's spirit goes to another world after death, even leaving briefly during sleep.

Left Villagers of the Cook Islands launch their outrigger canoe onto a lagoon. The Cook Islands are a far-flung group within Polynesia. They are mainly low-lying islands, surrounded by rich coral reefs and relying on coconut products for income. The Cook Islands have been self-governing since 1965, but New Zealand retains responsibility for defense and foreign affairs.

Left Surfers ride the waves along a beach in Guam, one of the Mariana Islands lying north of Micronesia. This Pacific island sport is many centuries old. The English explorer, Captain James Cook, described it in the 1770s.

THE COUNTRIES OF THE PACIFIC

78
Australia

80
New Zealand

82
Fiji, Kiribati, Nauru, Papua New Guinea, Solomon Islands, Tonga, Tuvalu, Vanuatu, Western Samoa

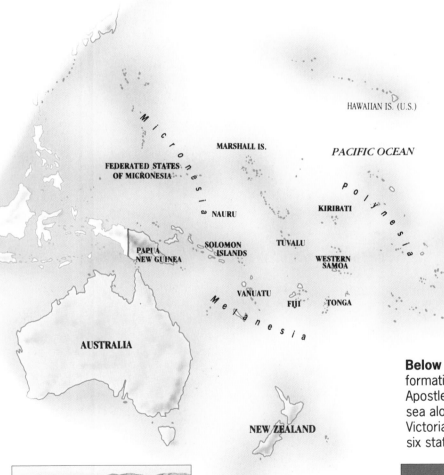

HAWAIIAN IS. (U.S.)

MARSHALL IS.

PACIFIC OCEAN

M i c r o n e s i a

FEDERATED STATES OF MICRONESIA

P o l y n e s i a

NAURU

KIRIBATI

PAPUA NEW GUINEA

SOLOMON ISLANDS

TUVALU

WESTERN SAMOA

VANUATU

FIJI

TONGA

M e l a n e s i a

AUSTRALIA

NEW ZEALAND

Below These dramatic rock formations, called the Twelve Apostles, were carved by the sea along the coast of Victoria, one of Australia's six states.

Left Neat rows of vines extend along the valley floor at Nelson, on New Zealand's South Island. The soil and mild climate of Australia and New Zealand are well suited to cultivating the grape vines that are best for producing wine. Increased wine production in both countries has helped their economies.

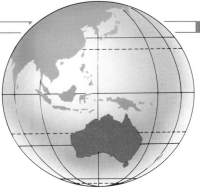

Left Sydney Opera House rises up from the harbor of Australia's largest city. Its graceful roof echoes the shape of the many boats that sail past it.

Below Ayers Rock, in central Australia, towers 984 ft (300 m) high and 1.5 miles (2.4 km) long. It is the world's largest rock. Its caves contain ancient Aboriginal paintings.

AUSTRALIA

Australia is the only country that is also a continent. Two thirds of Australia receives very little rain, so most Australians live on the fertile strip of land that runs along the eastern and southeastern coasts. The sparsely populated northeast is the wettest part of Australia. This area even has jungles and rain forests.

A chain of mountains called the Great Dividing Range separates the eastern coastal plains from Australia's dry interior, much of which is desert. This "outback" cannot support crops, but there are large sheep and cattle ranches, called stations. The few people who live in the outback lead isolated lives. They communicate with their neighbors by radio.

Australia is divided into six states and two territories. Tasmania, an island state off the southeast coast, has a cooler, wetter climate than the rest of the country.

It is rich in natural resources such as iron ore, coal, and silver. A large amount of raw materials is exported, providing Australia with its major source of wealth. Wool and meat are important exports, too.

Australia has many animals and plants that exist nowhere else. Among these are the kangaroo, wallaby, koala, and duck-billed platypus, a mammal that lays eggs.

Rainbows under the sea

The Great Barrier Reef extends 2,000 miles (3,200 km) along the northeast coast of Australia. The warm sunlit water is an ideal habitat for coral polyps, tiny marine animals only a tenth of an inch (a few millimetres) across. The polyps secrete coral, or limestone skeletons that link the animals together to form colonies. New layers of coral are added by each generation, often producing unusual and exotic shapes such as fans, domes or antlers.

Long-distance house calls

Many Australian cattle stations are more than a 10-hour drive from the nearest city or town. They rely on radio contact with doctors who can fly in for emergency medical care. This "flying doctor" service has operated since 1928. It is free to users, with costs covered by donations and funding by all of the six Australian states.

AUSTRALIA
Capital: Canberra
Population: 17,486,300

Left Kangaroos live only in Australia. They are called marsupials, which means that they carry their young in pouches. Their powerful hind legs are adapted to long journeys between far-flung watering holes in the outback. An adult kangaroo can reach speeds of 36 miles per hour (60 km/hr) and clear fences that are 10 ft (3 m) high.

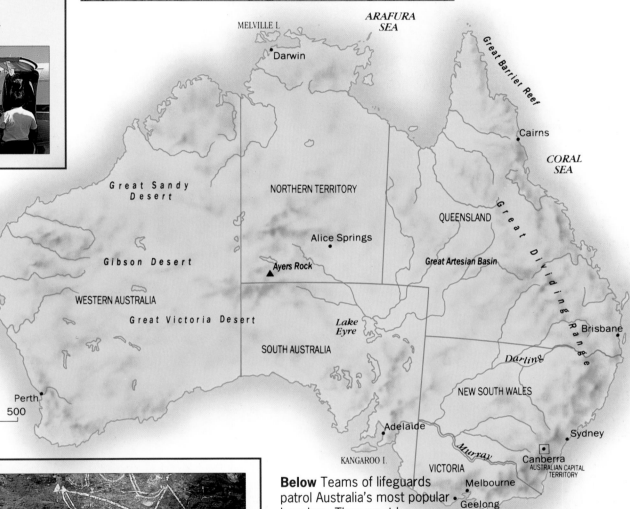

Below Teams of lifeguards patrol Australia's most popular beaches. They must be powerful swimmers who are able to cope with heavy surf, poisonous bites, and even sharks. Competitions keep their skills sharp.

The first Australians

There are about 227,000 Aborigines in Australia now. They probably came to Australia about 40,000 years ago, when Australia was joined to southeast Asia by a land bridge.

Aborigines believe in a process of creation known as Dreamtime, in which the Earth and all the plants and animals must be looked after. Aboriginal art often shows scenes and characters from Dreamtime.

NEW ZEALAND

New Zealand is a country consisting of dozens of islands lying about 1,000 miles (1,600 km) southeast of Australia. Most New Zealanders live on the two main islands, North Island and South Island. New Zealand also looks after the defense and foreign affairs of several groups of neighboring islands in the Pacific.

New Zealand is a country of dramatic and unspoiled scenery. Most of North Island consists of forests, pastures, and citrus orchards. In the center of the island is a large plateau with active volcanoes, hot springs, and geysers. South Island is more mountainous, with glaciers and snowcapped peaks towering above thick, green forests and sparkling lakes. In the east of South Island lie the Canterbury Plains, New Zealand's largest area of flat land and the country's chief grain-growing region.

New Zealand's mild, moist climate has made farming the main economic activity. Livestock are so numerous that for every person there are two head of cattle and twenty sheep! New Zealand lamb, butter, cheese, beef, and wool are exported around the world. Forestry, fishing, manufacturing, and tourism help to ensure that New Zealand does not depend too heavily on farming. Auckland, the country's largest city, is the main manufacturing center.

Below Wellington, the capital of New Zealand, is built around a fine harbor at the southern tip of North Island. While the port of Auckland handles most of the country's foreign trade, Wellington has all the traffic between the islands.

Above Sheep shearing is an important and marketable skill in New Zealand, which relies heavily on exports of wool and lamb. Shearers are often paid by the number of sheep shorn, rather than by the hour. An experienced shearer can trim a sheep in less than a minute.

Left Sheep are rounded into a pen in a farm in Queenstown, on New Zealand's South Island. New Zealand's mild, moist climate allows grass to grow all year, providing sheep with rich grazing land. More than half of New Zealand's total land area is devoted to sheep farming.

Maoris

The 250,000 Maoris in New Zealand are descendants of Polynesians who came from eastern Pacific islands about 700 years ago. They resisted European settlement in New Zealand, and their population declined to less than 50,000 at the end of the last century. Maoris remain proud of their heritage but have adapted to modern society.

Letting off steam

Geysers are common in the volcanic regions of New Zealand's North Island particularly around the area of Rotorua. These dramatic jets of water are produced by conditions like those of a pressure cooker. The water underground is heated by molten rock to more than 300°F (150°C), but the pressure from the surface water prevents it from boiling. If some of the surface water runs off or evaporates, the superheated water responds to the drop in pressure by immediately boiling up out of the funnel. The water is sent up to 230 ft (70 m) out of the ground.

NEW ZEALAND
Capital: Wellington
Population: 3,430,000

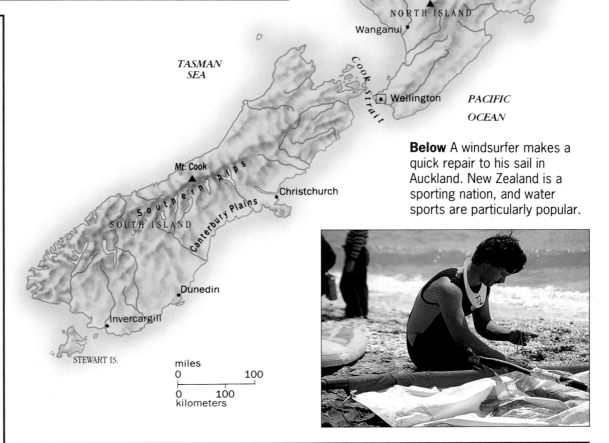

Auckland
Tauranga
Hamilton · Bay of Plenty
Rotorua
Lake Taupo
Mt. Ruapehu ▲
NORTH ISLAND
Wanganui ·

TASMAN SEA

Cook Strait
□ Wellington · PACIFIC OCEAN

Mt. Cook ▲
Southern Alps
Christchurch
SOUTH ISLAND · Canterbury Plains

· Dunedin

· Invercargill

STEWART IS.

miles
0 · 100
0 · 100
kilometers

Below A windsurfer makes a quick repair to his sail in Auckland. New Zealand is a sporting nation, and water sports are particularly popular.

A tough team to tackle

The All Blacks, pictured here playing England in the 1991 World Cup, are New Zealand's national rugby team. Rugby is the national sport, and there is fierce competition for places on the team. The All Blacks have been one of the world's leading rugby teams for more than 20 years. Their serious approach to the game is evident from the moment they take to the field.

THE PACIFIC ISLANDS

There are about 25,000 islands scattered over the Pacific Ocean, but only a few thousand are inhabited. The smallest are reefs that barely rise above sea level and form hazards for ships. The islands are split into three main groups – Melanesia, Micronesia, and Polynesia. Together they are called Oceania. The islands of Melanesia lie in the southwestern Pacific. The name Melanesia means "black islands," so called because many of these islanders have black skin. Micronesia, straddling the Equator to the north, means "small islands," while Polynesia, in the east, means "many islands."

There are two main types of Pacific island. Some, such as the islands of Tonga, Fiji, and Tahiti are mountainous. They are made of extinct or dormant volcanoes. Others are low-lying and built of coral.

Fiji, Kiribati, Nauru, Papua New Guinea, Solomon Islands, Tonga, Tuvalu, Vanuatu, and Western Samoa are all independent nations. The rest are controlled by other nations such as the United States, Britain, and France.

Palm-fringed beaches and the tropical climate attract tourists to many Pacific islands. Others, such as New Caledonia, Papua New Guinea, Fiji, and Nauru, export minerals. But many island people are poor. They build their own houses out of local materials and grow their own food. The main industries are fishing and agriculture.

Below Belau is the name of a group of lush Pacific islands in western Micronesia.

Above Hundreds of tribes, each with its own language, live in Papua New Guinea. The Melpa, pictured here, are a farming people who take great pride in their domesticated pigs and other livestock.

Above These young Solomon Islanders have the dark skin that gave Melanesia its name. The Solomon Islands lie east of Papua New Guinea. They rely on fishing and coconuts for their income.

The newest Pacific islands

The Lau are a Melanesian people who live on Malaita, one of the Solomon Islands lying east of Papua New Guinea. Some of their religious traditions have been almost untouched by Western influences. Certain Lau rituals mimic the natural forces of the world around them. Foueda is an example of a coral island created by humans. About the size of a tennis court, it is one of 60 artificial islands that the Lau have built. Men are forbidden from some of these islands, and women from the others, because Lau men and women live separately.

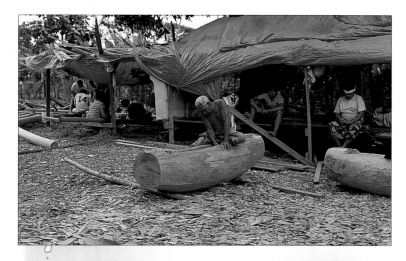

Left Traditional Polynesian boat-building methods are still used in parts of Samoa. Few other Pacific islands have the native hardwoods to withstand the sea and sun. A craftsman carves a log into the general shape of the boat before hardening it with a flaming torch. This process continues until the boat gradually achieves its final shape.

FIJI
Capital: Suva
Population: 772,000

KIRIBATI
Capital: Bairiki
Population: 69,000

NAURU
Capital: Yaren
Population: 9,000

PAPUA NEW GUINEA
Capital: Port Moresby
Population: 3,630,000

SOLOMON ISLANDS
Capital: Honiara
Population: 314,000

TONGA
Capital: Nuku'alofa
Population: 108,000

TUVALU
Capital: Funafuti
Population: 9,000

VANUATU
Capital: Vila
Population: 150,000

WESTERN SAMOA
Capital: Apia
Population: 169,000

MICRONESIA

HAWAIIAN IS.

MARSHALL IS.

PACIFIC OCEAN

FEDERATED STATES OF MICRONESIA

MELANESIA

POLYNESIA

NAURU

KIRIBATI

PAPUA NEW GUINEA

SOLOMON IS.

TUVALU

WESTERN SAMOA

VANUATU

FIJI

TONGA

AUSTRALIA

NEW ZEALAND

Jewels from the ocean floor

The warm waters around many Pacific islands are natural habitats for oysters and other mollusks that produce valuable pearls. (Pearl Harbor in the state of Hawaii, is named after the pearl beds that once flourished there.) Most pearls are still recovered in the traditional way, with divers slowly scouring the seabed with very little equipment. Experienced pearl divers can stay underwater for minutes at a time.

Right Easter Island is a remote island about 2,300 miles (3,700 km) west of Chile. Giant stone statues, called moai, stare out to sea. Some of them are more than 19 ft (6 m) high. Archaeologists believe the statues were built to honor the islanders' ancestors, who arrived at Easter Island by sea.

SECTION 8: THE POLES

The polar regions are sometimes called "Earth's Last Frontier." Their forbidding climates and long periods of darkness made them unknown territory until early in this century.

THE POLAR EXTREMES

At the far north and far south of the Earth lie the cold polar regions of the Arctic and the Antarctic. In these places, the sun does not rise for six months of every year. For the other six months, the sun never sets.

The Arctic lies north of the imaginary line known as the Arctic Circle. The North Pole itself is in the middle of the frozen ice cap of the Arctic Ocean. The northernmost regions of Europe, Asia, and North America border the Arctic Ocean. Few trees grow in the extreme north, but there is low grassland known as tundra. Here, snow and ice melt in the summer, and the climate is warm enough for plants to grow.

The continent of Antarctica is the coldest region on earth. It is larger than Europe and is surrounded by ocean. Ninety-nine percent of Antarctica lies permanently under ice, some of which is almost three miles thick. Scientists estimate that if all this ice were to melt because of global warming, the level of the world's oceans would rise by about 160 feet (48.7 m). There is no plant or animal life in the vast interior of Antarctica, but certain penguin species breed on its northern coasts. The surrounding seas are rich in marine life.

Both the Arctic and the Antarctic are rich in mineral resources. Oil, gold, copper, and iron are mined in the Arctic, but mining is forbidden in the Antarctic. It is likely that the richest mineral deposits lie beneath several hundred yards of ice and so would be difficult to obtain, but scientists are also concerned that mining would damage the environment.

Above The North Pole is in the heart of the Arctic region, which contains the northern-most parts of Europe, North America, and Asia. It is part of the polar ice cap, which expands and shrinks according to the season. The ice cap melts to its smallest area during the Arctic summer, when the sun shines 24 hours a day.

Below Pack ice begins to clog the mouth of Disko Bay in Greenland at the outset of winter. Pack ice is a large area of floating ice formed over many years. Several pieces of pack ice will form a larger ice pack if driven together by wind or currents. Pack ice is a shipping hazard and closes many Arctic ports for the winter.

Cold, hard facts

A British Antarctic Survey research station (left) stands on Signy Island off the Antarctic coast. Antarctica was the last continent to be explored, and the first to be devoted to peaceful purposes only. The Antarctic Treaty, signed in 1959 by all countries with bases on the continent, pledged that no country would use Antarctica for commercial or military purposes. Scientific bases contribute valuable information about the Earth's climate and atmosphere. They monitor the condition of the Earth's ozone layer. Scientists on the bases must go for 11 months without outside contact. Supplies can only arrive during the one month of Antarctic summer.

Above The ice and snow of Antarctica form unusual shapes. The ice was formed many hundreds of years ago, when it fell as snow.

Below Unlike the Arctic area, Antarctica is a continent under its ice cap. Except for a few islands on the Antarctic Peninsula, the whole continent lies permanently buried under the ice. The South Pole lies near the center of this land mass.

Below Wildflowers add some bright color to the tundra around Lake Brucebyen in Greenland. Arctic tundra regions lie frozen for most of the year, but each spring and early summer they "come alive" for a short time. Flowers blossom and other vegetation ripens, attracting grazing animals such as elk and reindeer.

Above A colony of Adelie penguins gathers in the breeding season during the short Antarctic summer. Adelie penguins live most of the year on pack ice off Antarctica but each year walk up to 50 miles (80 km) across the continent to breed. Some of their breeding colonies contain up to 5 million penguins.

Extent of ice in winter

Extent of ice in summer

WEDDELL
SEA

ANTARCTICA
South Pole

ROSS SEA

SECTION 9: THE OCEANS

Seen from outer space the Earth looks like one big ocean, and the continents look like mere islands. More than two thirds of the surface of the Earth is covered by seawater.

THE SOURCE OF LIFE

Oceans and seas cover almost 71 percent of the Earth's surface. The oceans are really one giant ocean, but different areas of this world ocean are given separate names. The ocean floor is as varied and changeable as any land region. There are vast plains, steep cliffs, high mountain ranges, and deep valleys.

The largest and deepest ocean is the Pacific, which occupies almost one third of the total surface area of the Earth. The Mariana Trench, a Pacific valley lying east of the Philippines, is 5,973 feet (10,924 m) deep. On the western rim of the Pacific lies the Indian Ocean, which ranks third in size.

The world's second largest ocean, the Atlantic, stretches from the eastern side of

Above A fishing vessel undergoes repairs in Japan. The Japanese fishing fleet is the largest in the world, with an annual catch of nearly 13 million tons. Many ships can or freeze the fish on board.

Below Waves pound the shore of Brittany in northwest France. Heavy waves created by storms can damage buildings and cause floods, but the same force can be harnessed as a source of energy.

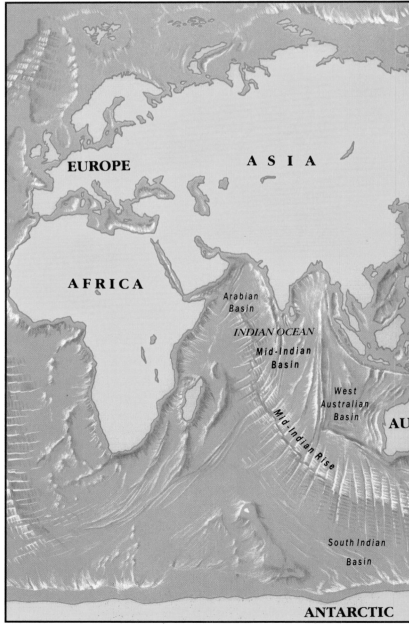

EUROPE

ASIA

AFRICA

Arabian Basin

INDIAN OCEAN

Mid-Indian Basin

West Australian Basin

AU

Mid Indian Rise

South Indian Basin

ANTARCTIC

North and South America to the west coasts of Europe and Africa. At its northern edge lies the Arctic Ocean, the world's smallest ocean. At the southern edge of the Atlantic is a vast area of water sometimes referred to as the Southern Ocean. This is not a separate ocean, but is made up of the waters of the Atlantic, the Pacific, and the Indian oceans.

The oceans are of great value. Seawater evaporates to form the atmosphere, which controls the Earth's climate and prevents it from becoming like that of Mars — blisteringly hot during the day and bitterly cold at night. The fish and other sea creatures that live in the oceans provide people with food. The power of the tides and waves can even be used to power generators and provide electricity.

Above Waste gas is burned away on an oil rig in the North Sea off Scotland. Until the 1960s nearly all of the world's oil came from land-based oil wells. The discovery of major oil and natural gas reserves in the North Sea led to new methods of drilling for oil. The results have been impressive. Oil and natural gas production have become important elements in the British and Norwegian economies.

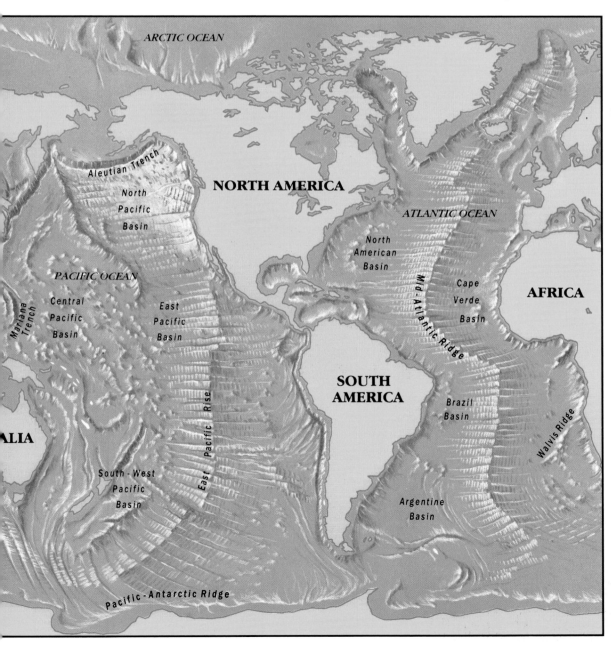

Above An aerial photograph shows the golden beaches that attract many tourists to Australia. Beautiful coral reefs lie off much of the Australian coastline.

Left A map of the world's oceans shows that the ocean floor has mountain ranges and valleys like those on the continents. Many of the Pacific islands are actually the crests of these underwater mountain ranges. Like famous mountain ranges on land, such as the Alps and the Andes, they were formed by movements in the Earth's crust. A narrow ledge of shallow water, called the continental shelf, forms the edge of most continents. Beyond lie many deep basins.

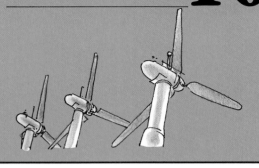

SECTION 10: A CHANGING WORLD

Droughts and floods are still common throughout the world but people have created a number of conditions to rival these natural disasters. Time is running out to solve some of these problems.

FACING THE PROBLEMS

The last decade of the 20th century has been a testing time for the world and its people. The environment has become "news," as each day's headlines tell us more about the "greenhouse effect," polluted rivers, and the destruction of the Amazon rain forest.

Thousands of years of scientific progress should have taught people how to address problems such as floods, droughts, and hurricanes. Instead, these natural disasters still take their dreadful toll, accepted by many as a fact of life. Rather than solving these age-old problems, modern society has merely added to the list of trouble spots.

Progress in science and industry has led to polluted air and water, as well as soil robbed of its nutrients. Aerosols, commercial aircraft, and refrigerators widen the hole in the ozone layer. Some cities have even run out of room to dispose of their rubbish.

The people of the late 20th century need imagination and resolve to reverse these destructive trends. Otherwise the people of the 21st century will never breathe clean air or drink pure water.

Above An airplane sprays crops on a large farm in Kenya. Aerial crop spraying is sometimes the only answer to the problems facing African farms. Insect pests such as locusts are as much a problem as the chronic droughts.

Above Cracked, parched earth is the stark proof of drought in Cyprus. Lack of regular rainfall is a problem faced by millions of farmers around the world. Some people blame a permanent change in climate.

Left Only stumps remain of trees that grew in this part of New South Wales, Australia. A combination of drought and over-farming destroys the topsoil and allows the desert to take over. Scientists call this process desertification.

A hole in the atmosphere

The ozone layer is part of the Earth's atmosphere. It protects the Earth by filtering out the harmful ultraviolet radiation from the sun. Too much of this type of radiation can give people skin cancer and even change the climate by affecting crops. The ozone layer is threatened by fluorocarbons, chemicals which are contained in aerosols and used by industry in other ways. Certain types of fertilizer may also affect the ozone layer. Studies of the atmosphere have contained alarming news. They have shown a hole in the ozone layer developing over Antarctica.

Right Uncontrolled heavy industry threatens the quality of life of people around the world. These Russians are sunbathing and swimming along the Dudinka river in Siberia. On the other bank lies Norilsk, an industrial city with some of Russia's largest copper refineries. The river and air are badly polluted but the people have nowhere else to go to relax.

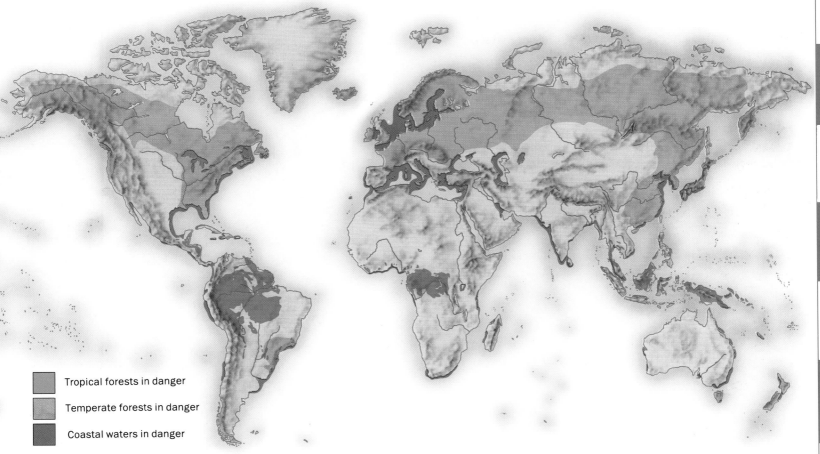

Tropical forests in danger

Temperate forests in danger

Coastal waters in danger

Above Heavy industry pollutes the air and sea in Europe, North America, and parts of Asia. Fishing and swimming have been ruined by sea pollution. The destruction of forests is a worldwide problem. Many forests in Europe and North America have already been cut down. Tropical rain forests in South America, Africa, and Australia are now threatened.

Victims of progress

The Yanomami are South American Indians who live in the rain forests of southern Venezuela and northern Brazil.
Until recently they have been protected by the remoteness of their scattered villages. But much of the surrounding rain forest has been cleared. The Yanomami have been forced from their homelands and hunting grounds. Soon there will be no more land for them. Their problems show that the destruction of the world's rain forests is a human tragedy as well as an environmental disaster.

THE FUTURE

Not all the news is bad for Planet Earth. Scientific progress and concern for the environment are improving the outlook for the 21st century. And many of our worst problems, such as droughts, floods, and fuel shortages, might be blessings in disguise. The solutions to some of these crises may benefit research in other areas where up to now there have been only difficulties.

The world experienced a shortage of oil and oil-related products in the 1970s. As a result, many countries began looking for alternative ways of supplying energy. More money was pumped into research.

Some of the proposed solutions, such as solar power and nuclear fusion, represented new forms of energy supplies. Others, including large-scale windmills and tidal-powered electrical generators, were new versions of old ideas. What they shared was the ability to conserve the Earth's resources while providing new sources of power.

Real travel will also be transformed in the future. Streamlined cars and trains will look

Recycling precious resources

For decades people, especially in the prosperous countries of the West, have thrown away products once they are finished. But scientists' messages have helped end this "throwaway society." Recycling centers have become common, as people realize that common items such as ring-pulls, bottle tops, and newspapers can be reprocessed. Certain household goods, such as aluminium, glass, and paper, are recycled very easily.

In the future more and more people will begin their recycling at home. Most of what is now considered trash will be collected in separate bags to go to different recycling centers. Scientists are constantly looking for methods of recycling other metals and textiles. Many more products will be made from recycled ingredients in the future. And evidence now suggests that recycling will no longer be seen as a sacrifice or a chore. Current trends show that the cost of finding new materials is rising faster than the cost of recycling the same items.

Powering the future

Energy is an area where the future will be very different from the present. Much of our energy is still derived from "fossils fuels" such as coal, oil, natural gas, and wood. These fuels are called "non-renewable" because we cannot create more coal, for example, to replace the coal we have mined and burned. New sources of energy are likely to be "renewable" and unlikely to be used up so easily. Already there have been experiments to produce energy from the wind and

Left Rows of windmills are positioned over open countryside in England.

like spaceships, while passenger aircraft will be able to travel from London to Sydney in four hours — less than one fifth of the time it takes today.

All these exciting pictures of the future depend on our ability to preserve the Earth's resources. The forms of energy we develop to replace wasteful fossil fuels will also be more efficient — and cheaper. Countries now suffering droughts may be able to use the sun to power irrigation projects in the future. Tidal power may provide power for countries that now live in fear of floods.

Tuning in to tomorrow

The "communications revolution" of the last 30 years is likely to continue into the next century. Each year brings new discoveries to improve the ways in which we send and receive information. Telephones linked by wires will become a thing of the past as fiber-optic technology and satellite links replace old connections. Computers will continue to speed up communications so that people in several parts of the world will be able to see each other and hold a conversation.

Above A satellite dish picks up signals on a Hawaiian hillside, while visual display units provide news on the streets of Sydney (below).

Transportation for the future

Sleek design will enable vehicles to use less energy while traveling at greater speed. They will hold more passengers. And transportation of all types will begin to use fuels that do not pollute the air and water.

Below These Latvian schoolchildren are planting saplings in an area where many trees had been cut down for the lumber industry. Northern Europe and Scandinavia are rich in the trees used to make timber and paper. Proper forest management is a type of recycling. A constant supply of new trees can replace those that have been used for industry. These trees will be cut when these children are older, but other trees will replace them.

Above Solar panels in Kenya provide the power to pump water for irrigation projects.

the sea. Areas with constant winds can use windmills to power electricity generators. The power of ocean waves and tides can also be harnessed. Sunshine is another likely power source. Solar panels can absorb the warmth from sunshine to heat water and to provide electricity.

INDEX

ACKNOWLEDGEMENTS

Quarto would like to thank the following for providing photographs, and for granting permission to reproduce copyright material.

Australian Tourist Commission: 78br, 87cr; Austrian National Tourist Office: 23br; Lucy Byrne: 63bl; Nick Buzzard: 6bl, 62ar, 62bl, 64cr, 65c, 66cl, 90bl; Chris Christodoulou: 18bc; Moira Clinch: 36br; CM Dixon: 81ac; Abbie Enock: 34cr, 60cr; Finnish Tourist Board: 31al; Jimmy Holmes: 26bl, 32ac, 35al, 41ac, 42cr, 45br; Hutchison: 10cl, 10bc, 11al, 11ar, 15bl, 18cr, 19bl, 20al, 21br, 24cr, 27ar, 28ar, 29ar, 36cr, 37bl, 40bl, 41bl, 42al, 43cr, 43bc, 44bl, 45bl, 47c, 47br, 49c, 53ar, 53bc, 54cr, 56cr, 56bl, 58c, 59br, 61al, 61bc, 63br, 64br, 65bl, 68ar, 68br, 69cr, 69bc, 70cr, 71ac, 71br, 73cl, 73c, 75c, 75cr, 76cr, 77a, 78cr, 80cr, 81cr, 82cr, 82bl, 83br, 86cl, 86bl, 88cr, 89br, 91ar; Anthony Lambert: 32bc, 33al, 33bl; Landform Slides: 30bl; Life File: 8br, 9br, 14bl, 15cr, 16ar, 16bl, 17c, 18ar, 19al, 20cr, 28br, 29br, 30cr, 32cr, 38cr, 39al, 45ac, 46bl, 47bc, 49a, 59cr, 59bc, 65al, 68cr, 69cl, 72cr, 75ac, 77br, 78al, 79ac, 80ar, 90cr; Millership: 38br; NASA: 63ar; Panos Pictures: 48cr, 49bl, 50ar, 52cr, 57br, 79bl; South African Tourist Board: 57bl; Travel Photo International: 16br; Trip: Alison Bradley 44cr; Igor Burgandinov 37a; Joan Batten 54ar, 74cr; Colin Conway 54br; T Davies 9br; Eye Ubiquitous 13al, 14bc, 16cr, 21al, 22ar, 22br, 22bl, 23bl, 27cl, 34bl, 35c, 59ar, 69cr, 71br, 81br, 87ar, 91cl; C Farndon 53al; R Farrier Smith 65ar; Leslie Garland 19ac; Andrew Gasson 32br, 67ar, 85c; Juliet Highet 52bl; Linda Jackson 12al; Andrzej Jarosvewicz 33br; Victor Kolpakov 15br, 91br; Alexander Kuznetsov 33cr, 89a; Life File 58bl, 63c, 72br, 83al, 85al; Jaroslav Novotny 24bc; Mike Portelly 67cr; Richard Powers 66br, 72bl; Norman Price 8ar, 61ac, 84br, 85bl; Chris Rennie 26cr; Roy Robertson 21bl; Helene Rogers 7ar, 9ar, 13al, 24br, 27bl, 27br, 34br, 35bl, 39bc, 40cr, 43cl, 46ar, 48bl, 50cr, 51al, 51bl, 55ac, 67c, 74bl, 88c, 88bl, 91cr; Pete Sanders 46cr; Dave Saunders 24cl, 30cr, 49br, 50bl, 54bl, 55bl, 56br, 73br, 75br, 75bl, 76bl, 79cl; Howard Sayer 7al; RH Seale 37br; Sefton Photo Library 58cr, 59al, 60al, 61br, 63c, 64bl, 71bl, 85cr; George Spencley 62cr; Roy Styles 17bl, 20br, 31br; Bob Turner 6br, 14al; Joan Wakelin 44br, 47cl, 77bl, 79br, 80bl; David Williamson 25bl, 25br; Tony Waltham 39bl.

(a = above, b = bottom, c = center, l = left, r = right)

Whilst every effort has been made to trace and acknowledge all copyright holders, we would like to apologize should any omissions have been made.